"A beautifully told story that will inspire every family to deeper faith."
— Jennifer Fulwiler, radio host and author of *One Beautiful Dream:
The Rollicking Tale of Family Chaos, Personal Passions,
and Saying Yes to Them Both*

"Of all the biographical works about Fulton Sheen I've read, Bonnie Engstrom's *61 Minutes To a Miracle* is by far the best. Her account of Sheen's intercession through Christ in literally raising her son James Fulton from the dead is impossible, of course. Except that it happened. Engstrom is not only a woman of faith but a writer's writer who manages to infuse a harrowing tale — every parent's worst nightmare — with dreamlike joy. By God's grace, this deceptively small book has the power to touch hearts and minds."
— Patrick Coffin, Host, *The Patrick Coffin Show*

"As a saint lover, I've read many stories about miraculous healings, but this might be the most incredible. It's perhaps more intriguing given that it happened in our own time. ... It's hard (if not impossible) to explain little James's healing without divine intervention. That's why seven medical experts reviewing this case, some non-Catholic, unanimously agreed there was no natural explanation. The theological experts agreed the healing should be attributed to the intercession of Fulton Sheen. ... But Bonnie Engstrom's account in this book is more than just a shocking miracle story. It's also, as are the best miracle stories, an uplifting and encouraging testament to the ways God and his saints continue to work in this world. If you have friends or family who don't believe in God, or doubt there are forces in this world beyond the merely material, this book may change their minds."
— Brandon Vogt, founder of ClaritasU
and author of *Why I Am Catholic*

"It's easy (and maybe comfortable) to confine the earth-shattering, world-changing-type miracles to back in ye olde Bible days. But James Fulton Engstrom's life is a testament to the fact that BIG important miracles can happen in our time, in regular homes, to normal families. His mom's lovely little book gives us all a fascinating window into one family's experience living through — and with — a Church-approved, doctor-verified medical miracle!"

— Kendra Tierney, mother of many, blogger, author of *The Catholic All Year Compendium*

"Do you believe in miracles? You will after reading this book. ... I've had the double pleasure of reading about this story and meeting Bonnie Engstrom and her husband, Travis. What happened with their stillborn son, James Fulton, with the intercession of Fulton Sheen, is quite literally amazing, extraordinary — miraculous. What happened to James Fulton, well, just doesn't happen. It was, in fact, a certified miracle credited to the late, great Bishop Fulton Sheen."

— Paul Kengor, PhD, professor of political science, Grove City College, author of *A Pope and a President*

"Bonnie, Travis, and James's story is an incredible witness to our Lord's faithfulness, His never-ending love for us, and His desire to pour His grace into every crevice of our lives. If you don't believe in miracles, this book is for you. Prepare to be astonished. If you already believed in miracles, this book will deepen your faith in a mighty God who saves."

— Jenna Guizar, founder and creative director of Blessed Is She, Inc.

61 Minutes to a Miracle

61 MINUTES
TO A
Miracle

FULTON SHEEN AND A
TRUE STORY OF THE IMPOSSIBLE

BONNIE L. ENGSTROM

Our Sunday Visitor
Huntington, Indiana

Our Sunday Visitor Publishing Division
Our Sunday Visitor, Inc.
200 Noll Plaza
Huntington, IN 46750
www.osv.com
1-800-348-2440

ISBN: 978-1-61278-717-6 (Inventory No. T1421)
eISBN: 978-1-61278-327-7
LCCN: 2019942862

Cover and interior design: Lindsey Riesen
Cover art: Shutterstock.com and Stephanie Zimmerman

PRINTED IN THE UNITED STATES OF AMERICA

"When Jesus heard it he said, 'This illness is not unto death; it is for the glory of God, so that the Son of God may be glorified by means of it.'"

John 11:4, The Story of Lazarus

CONTENTS

INTRODUCTION

Growing up on the South Side of Chicago, I had several constants in my life: Eisenhower was president. Pius was pope. Mom and Dad were in charge. And Fulton Sheen was on television. Like most Catholics of my generation, I felt almost as if Bishop Sheen were part of our family — after all, he was in our living room every week!

When I became the bishop of Peoria in 2002, I was soon approached by the leaders of the Archbishop Fulton John Sheen Foundation, asking me to become the sponsor of the cause for Sheen's canonization. Less than six months after taking my seat in the cathedral of Peoria, I was privileged to convene the canonical tribunal that would investigate Sheen's life and legacy. I personally set out to reread every Sheen book I could get my hands on, having first read them many years ago. I truly became steeped in everything "Sheen" — not just his incredible spiritual and academic legacy, but also his Midwest roots, which I was reminded of everywhere I went. You can't throw a stone in central Illinois and not hit someone who is related to Fulton Sheen! Further,

I live in his childhood neighborhood. The cathedral, attached to my residence, was where young Fulton made his First Holy Communion and was an altar boy. The building that was his high school is a block away and is part of our diocesan pastoral center. His parents and grandparents are buried in our cathedral cemetery. And, of course, the high altar before which Sheen was ordained a priest and offered his first Solemn Mass still adorns our beautiful Cathedral of Saint Mary of the Immaculate Conception.

While the historical and theological investigations into Sheen's life and teaching progressed, we also encouraged Catholics around the world to ask God to work a miracle through Sheen's intercession. Letters poured in from around the world, detailing moving accounts of "little" miracles — many prayers answered, including healings of body and soul. As vice-postulator, Father Andrew Apostoli, CFR, was responsible for following up on these reported miracles. He would captivate me at our regular meetings with some truly incredible accounts. Eventually, we had multiple reported miracles that warranted a full investigation by Church authorities. Each one seemed more incredible than the last. If there are levels of the miraculous, it was almost as if "Someone" was shouting from heaven, louder and louder!

Until …

The account contained in this book relates a miracle of near biblical proportions. It is also a story of a family's faith, the power of prayer, and the fruit of trustful surrender to God. As there are no "accidents" with God, I believe that part of the providential nature of this moving account is that it happened in Fulton Sheen's hometown, within view of the spires of his cathedral-parish. I was honored to be the bishop tasked by the Church to investigate Sheen's life of heroic virtue. I am amazed to be the bishop who had the privilege to preside over the diocesan tribunal that investigated this verified miracle.

Only God performs miracles. Only the Church can declare a miracle. Only God makes saints, and in his own time. Fulton Sheen, help us!

+ Daniel R. Jenky

The Most Reverend Daniel R. Jenky, CSC
Bishop of Peoria
President, Archbishop Fulton John Sheen Foundation

CHAPTER 1

First Impressions

Growing up in central Illinois, I had heard the name *Bishop Sheen* multiple times, usually from my grandparents. But the first time I saw him, I was sitting in my parents' living room, home from college on summer break. As I flipped through the TV, I paused for a moment on the Catholic television network to look back at the man whose eyes pierced the screen and looked right at me.

"Who's that?" I asked my mom as she walked through the room.

"That's Bishop Sheen. He's from around here. He was born in El Paso, I think," she said.

His deep, dark eyes stared as his hand grabbed the edge of his long cape, dramatically flared it out, and pulled it to the front of his chest. His cheeks were hollow; his face was thin; he was passionate about something.

"He looks like a vampire," I replied, curling my lip. My mom chuckled and kept walking. I shook my head and changed the channel. I wasn't interested in what a spooky-looking priest had to say about God.

Little did I know that ten years later, after a beautiful, calm labor and delivery, I would kneel on my bedroom floor, holding the newborn baby we had named for Bishop Sheen. I would look at my husband who, with tears in his eyes, gazed at the still, quiet, blue baby in my arms. Little did I know that the man I had snubbed as a college student would be the same one who would walk with my family and me in the longest, hardest moments of my life.

CHAPTER 2

Love, Marriage, and a Baby
in a Baby Carriage

I met Travis on my first day of work at the Saint Francis of Assisi Catholic Student Center. I was a recent college graduate, and he was a super senior who did maintenance at St. Francis in exchange for room and board. He was strong, tan, and handsome. He was also still in love with his ex-girlfriend, so we spent our day cleaning, rearranging furniture, and talking about her.

Over the next two years, our friendship grew. Every day we saw each other, worked together, and chatted. Meanwhile, he got back together with his girlfriend, who became his fiancée, and I went on dates with various men, none of whom met Travis's approval. But as my best friends left for convents, I relied on my friendship with Travis more and more. He was kind and gentle and not afraid of hard work. He treated me and every woman with respect, and he made me laugh. It wasn't long before I realized that he was one of my best friends and one of the people I respected most in life.

As our friendship deepened, Travis felt a growing tug toward the priesthood. In the spring of my second year at St. Francis, he ended his engagement so he could more seriously discern life as a religious or diocesan priest. I was nothing but proud of him, and cheered him on.

For weeks, Travis daily went to the chapel and asked God, "What do you want me to do with my life?" While he was asking about routes to the priesthood, the day came when God clearly answered. But instead of a collar, God showed him me. I knew nothing of this answered prayer, but it wasn't long after that I realized I was in love with Travis. Over the two years our friendship had grown in love, respect, and admiration, and once we individually realized what had happened, we came together to discuss it. Two weeks later we had a wedding date selected; four weeks after that there was a ring on my finger, and wedding plans moved ahead. Six months later, we were married.

We honeymooned in Scotland, where I quoted *Braveheart* in a ridiculously bad accent while Travis drove us through the gorgeous countryside. Once we returned home, we went to the movies, drove Travis's 1969 Chevelle with the windows down to and from the ice cream shop, and rode our bikes on country roads. Soon we bought a fixer-upper and began daily trips to various home improvement stores.

Five months after our wedding, I took a pregnancy test. Positive. We were thrilled and scared and all the feelings that come to first-time parents. But within the week the small baby had died, and I spent my first Mother's Day miscarrying. In my grief I read every baby book I could get my hands on. My obstetrician's bedside manner was lacking as I cried over the lost pregnancy, so I found myself more and more drawn to books about homebirth. The authors, midwives, and homebirth community seemed to respect life, pregnancy, babies, women's bodies, and motherhood in a way that I had not encountered at my ob/gyn's office. They validated my grief and the love I felt for the child I had lost. So, when I found myself pregnant again, Travis and I met with a homebirth midwife. By the end of our interview, we knew we wanted her to be the one to deliver the baby, and that we would do so from the comfort of our own home.

My pregnancy with Lydia and her homebirth were perfect, and when I found myself pregnant with Bennet, we continued with the same midwife. Travis and I enjoyed being home, eating birthday cake and watching the Jason Bourne movies together while snuggling with our babies.

CHAPTER 3

Gifts from God

B efore I knew I was pregnant with my fourth child, I sat with my spiritual director, Father Joseph Donton, and confided in him that I never wanted to be pregnant again. After two full-term babies and one miscarriage in just three years of marriage, I was done with being open to life. Leaning back in his chair, he asked me, "If you found out today that you were pregnant, what would you say?"

I looked him in the eye and snarled, "Oh, shit!"

He laughed at my honesty and told me that we needed to work on that attitude.

Just a week later, my daughter, not yet two, played in the living room, running circles around my three-month-old son. Bennet cooed and laughed; Lydia ran and danced and sang, occasionally kissing him. It was how they usually played, when Lydia wasn't ignoring him completely.

In the next room, I sat on the edge of my bed and looked at

the pregnancy test I held in my hand. I looked out the window and looked back at the test. It was positive, and while I wasn't surprised, I was definitely ... surprised. My husband, Travis, and I were so tired and so busy adjusting to life as a family of four that we didn't feel called to do anything other than get out of bed every morning, let alone have another baby.

We were already living paycheck to paycheck. We were already getting by on less sleep than we would have liked. We were already cramming car seats into the back of a tiny two-door Chevy.

I looked out the window again and gave up. "Okay, God. I believe this baby is a gift. I believe you want this baby to exist. You're going to have to provide." I didn't say "or else," but it was implied. I wasn't making a statement of faith; I was letting him know that I was holding him accountable.

But provide he did.

For starters, my pregnancy was super easy. There was barely any morning sickness. Mild gestational diabetes was controlled through diet; and in every other way, the baby and I were completely healthy. And the icing on the cake: I was able to nap almost every day.

Then one afternoon a gas card arrived in the mail from an anonymous sender. Soon after, someone offered to buy us a new sofa so we could get rid of the hand-me-down sinking pit that sat in our living room. Next, a friend of the family sent us a new laptop, knowing that Travis had returned to school for his master's degree. Right after that, our midwife explained that we did not owe her $500 as we believed, but that the previous birth had been covered in full by insurance. And then there was the cash.

One month after my visit with Father Donton, I returned and told him that I had, in fact, been pregnant during our previous meeting. Remembering our last conversation, he laughed and asked me what I had said when I found out. I told him that Travis and I knew that God wanted the baby to exist, and that we were excited to find out why. I told him that we were trusting God to provide for us, and that so far he had been very generous. Father cocked his head a bit and looked at me from the other side of his desk. "It's interesting that you say that, because I have something I need to give you," he said. "Wait here a moment."

He left the room, returning a few minutes later with a white envelope in hand. "A member of the congregation gave me a large sum of money," he said. "He and his wife wanted to help someone in need, but they didn't know who that would be. They figured that people come to church and ask for help, and that I would know when to give it out. So I'm giving half of it to you. I think the Holy Spirit wants you to have it."

I stood there, with wide eyes and gaping mouth. I stammered out a "Thank you" as he handed me the envelope.

We confirmed our next meeting and said goodbye, and I headed to my car. After I slid behind the wheel, I peeked into the envelope. Ben Franklin was looking at me with his droopy eyes as I counted five crisp bills.

I was amazed. Five hundred dollars is a lot of money to most people, but to my family it is a *lot* of money. I drove home, shaking my head in grateful wonder. As I approached my house, I pulled up to the mailbox. I parked, sifted through the mail, and opened the one bill in the stack. Our biannual car insurance payment was due, and we owed $482. I broke into a huge, goofy grin. Not only did we have enough money to cover what is usually a difficult bill for us to pay, but we also had enough money left over to go out for ice cream! I was blown away by God's obvious provision and generosity.

CHAPTER 4

Choosing a Name

Travis and I were still discussing baby names when I was seven months pregnant. We were waiting until birth to learn the gender, but we knew that if the baby was a girl, she would be named Teresa Elizabeth. The boy's name, however, was undecided. I wanted to name my son Linus, but Travis strongly protested. I tried to point out that not many boys are named Linus, so the second pope was just sitting around in heaven with hardly anyone to pray for. I also explained that a boy named Linus would be sure to have a never-ending supply of blue security blankets. Travis rolled his eyes and said it wasn't going to happen.

In the midst of this ongoing bickering, Archbishop Fulton J. Sheen resurfaced in my life. As a volunteer for a local women's ministry, I had the task of applying for a grant named after the late archbishop. My only impression of the man was still that he looked like a vampire, so I wanted to know more about him and his mission before I begged for money from people who loved him.

My husband and I knew who Fulton Sheen was in a peripheral sense. Sheen's birthplace is twenty miles from our home, and he grew up in Peoria, very close to where we were both born and raised, and were raising our own family. We knew he had been a television personality in the 1950s. Aside from these facts, though, we knew very little of the man. Just as Nathaniel in the John's Gospel asked whether anything good could come out of Nazareth (cf. Jn 1:46), I wondered whether anything good could come out of El Paso, Illinois — a small, simple town that is no different from thousands of other lackluster small towns across the world.

But just like Nathaniel, I would soon learn that I was wrong.

One day I sat in front of the computer, watching YouTube videos as I continued my research. Fulton Sheen had once appeared on *What's My Line*, an old game show, and I called Travis over to watch with me. We were impressed by his humor and the way that everyone clearly liked him. The people on the show obviously respected Bishop Sheen and enjoyed being in his presence. We were shocked; never had we seen a Catholic figure so well received in a secular setting. Obviously, there was much more to the man than we thought.

We watched old videos posted on the internet, listening to him preach. We read about him on blogs and websites. Again and again, we were blown away by how intelligent and yet approachable he was. His face wasn't foreboding like I had remembered. His broad smile was sincere, and he told jokes and funny stories, often at his own expense. I was especially drawn to how he spoke about children; it was obvious that he respected and appreciated them. Fulton Sheen was funny, articulate, and clearly loved Jesus Christ and his Church. Turning to my husband, I said: "His cause for canonization is open. This man is gonna be a saint someday."

We decided then that if the child I was carrying was a boy, we would name him after Fulton Sheen. Soon enough we settled on the name James Fulton, a way to honor Travis's brother and Saint James the Greater, as well as our new friend, Bishop Sheen.

After that day we began asking for Sheen's intercession. We still didn't know whether the baby would be a boy or girl but suspected that he was a boy. Most mornings when I prayed, I would reach out to Bishop Sheen and ask him to pray for my pregnancy, for a short and easy labor and delivery, and for a healthy baby. I asked Sheen to follow my child through his life, constantly praying for him so that he would grow into a good man who loved God.

I knew that I could trust Sheen to take good care of my child. Midwesterners tend to be hardworking and kind, and Sheen was a local boy to boot! It felt good knowing that such a holy man was praying for my unborn baby.

CHAPTER 5

A Troubling Dream

At the beginning of my eighth month of pregnancy, I began to second-guess my decision to have another homebirth.

My first two homebirths had been wonderful experiences, even though the labors had been long. But as this pregnancy continued, I began to think that another homebirth was no longer the best decision. I was already exhausted from being pregnant while caring for two very little ones, and I worried that I would labor for another seventeen to twenty-one hours as I had with Lydia and Bennet. If that were the case, when the time came to push, I was afraid I wouldn't have it in me. I didn't want to jeopardize our baby's health or mine, so I brought my concerns to Travis, my midwife Bernice, and my mom. Mom liked the idea of the hospital, and Bernice was ready to support whichever decision I made. But Travis was convinced I had the strength of body and spirit and thought I should stay at home. He encouraged me to pray about it, so I did.

A few nights later, I had a dream. Even though Travis and I usually choose not to learn the gender of our unborn children, at that time I had always known what we were having because of my dreams. With Lydia I dreamed that I was holding and cuddling a newborn baby girl. The dream was lifelike, and the next morning I confidently told Travis that I was pregnant with a girl. Travis laughed; but when I had a lifelike dream that I gave birth to a baby boy while pregnant with Bennet, he didn't laugh again.

So by the time I was pregnant with James, Travis and I had started to take my baby-related dreams fairly seriously. But this dream was troubling, and I carried its heaviness with me throughout the next day, awaiting a chance to discuss it with my husband.

Finally, after eating dinner, cleaning the kitchen, and tucking in the kids, Travis and I crawled into our queen-sized bed. With his head on the white pillow and mine on his chest, we pulled the quilt up to our shoulders.

"Travis," I said to him, "I need to tell you something."

The look on his face showed that he knew I was serious, and even a little anxious. "Okay. What is it?"

"Last night I dreamt that here in our bedroom, in the middle of the floor, I gave birth to a baby boy. It was a completely normal dream — nothing weird or out of place. Actually, it was really lifelike."

He interrupted me and proudly said, "I knew we were having a boy!"

"Travis, in the dream he was blue; he wasn't alive. I dreamed

I gave birth to a stillborn."

Fear made his eyes widen slightly, and his mouth formed a silent, slow, "Oh." Then he softly said to me, "That can't happen."

"I know. I know."

We didn't talk about the dream again, choosing to ignore it, but deep down I couldn't shake it. Anxiety bundled and knotted in my shoulders and stomach, and it drove me to prayer time and time again, each time asking for God to make it obvious to me whether I should have my baby at home as I wanted, or plan on a hospital delivery.

In the end, I felt great peace about giving birth at home. It was the kind of peace that didn't come from me: I was confident that home was where God wanted us. I told Travis and Bernice that I would stay home for the labor and delivery, though if at any point I asked for a transfer to the hospital, they should take me there immediately.

The knots untangled, and my whole body relaxed into the last month of pregnancy. The baby was healthy, and I was in God's will. I was ready.

CHAPTER 6

The Cusp of Something Great

In mid-September, I woke up to my two-year-old daughter climbing into bed with me. Bleary-eyed, I noted that my husband had already left for work and my one-year-old son was still sleeping. I had had contractions through the night, but I was grateful that I had still been able to get in a good night's sleep. I snuggled up to my daughter, soaking up my last moments of laziness and calm before the new baby came.

By the time we were all out of bed and beginning our day, I was certain that The Day had arrived; I called my mom and asked her to come over. To keep the contractions going, I did every trick in the book: went for a walk, found every excuse possible to go up and down the stairs, scrubbed the bathtub, danced around the kitchen. When my husband got home from work, we climbed into his old Dodge and went for a drive, hitting every bump in the road. Thank God for potholes — by the time we got home, I was in real labor. After I updated Facebook and my blog with a request for prayers, we called Bernice, my mother-in-law, and a few friends who were coming to help with the labor and child care.

An hour later, I was laboring in front of the TV when Kim, Bernice's assistant, arrived. She firmly encouraged me to go on a walk to speed things up. I slipped on my flip-flops and went out the door, grabbing Travis's hand as I toddled down the porch steps.

Much to the embarrassment of my husband, my contractions seemed to come under every streetlight. Holding on to him, lit up for anyone who happened to glance out their window to see, I swayed my hips through each contraction. The walk was working, and my contractions were becoming longer, stronger, and closer together. As we approached the main door of the Apostolic Christian Church, which was filled for its Wednesday night service, my most intense contraction of the day hit, causing my water to break. Because we were under yet another streetlight, we were able to see that the fluid was clear, a reassuring sign of a healthy baby in what was otherwise an awkward situation.

Back at the house, Bernice had arrived and unloaded her medical supplies. She came out to the sidewalk to greet us and ask about my progress. We decided to head upstairs so I could continue laboring in my bedroom, the place I wanted to be for delivery. On my way up, I said goodbye to my mom, who wanted to get a good night's sleep before the baby came, and hello to our friend Katie and my mother-in-law, Deb, who had all arrived to help.

Bernice and Kim quickly prepared the bedroom. They turned off the overhead lights so that the only light breaking into the room came from the partially closed closet and hall doors. The dark and shadowy room was calm and relaxing for me. Unlike a hospital's labor and delivery room, there would be no glare, no stainless steel, and no stiff sheets and gowns. Bernice and Kim would time my contractions, follow my progress, and make handwritten notations on my charts by the glow of a flashlight.

In my own clothes, among my own things, I labored. A large cup my grandmother had given me held ice water and was within reach at all times. On top of our cluttered dresser were pictures of friends and family, including a black-and-white image of Archbishop Sheen, and knickknacks reminding us of our trips to Poland, Germany, Italy, and Scotland. The bassinette, covered in white eyelet, was tucked in a corner, with clean pajamas, receiving blankets, and small diapers stacked in its bottom storage basket. Flannel-backed vinyl tablecloths lay on the soft brown carpet, fuzzy side up. Fresh towels and absorbent mats were close at hand so they could be added as needed. Our perpetually unmade bed was also made waterproof, while piles of extra pillows and stacks of blankets were placed just so, allowing me to rest between contractions, positioned in a way to keep labor progressing.

Right away, Bernice brought out her handheld fetal Doppler and held it to my belly, carefully timing the heartbeats as they played out of the speaker for us all to hear. They were strong and steady, and sped up a little bit during my contractions, just like they were supposed to. Knowing that my baby was healthy and that medical professionals were with me, I relaxed into the labor. The pain grew more intense, but I combatted it by swaying my hips as I knelt, breathing deeply, and clinging to my husband's strong shoulders. Kim and Bernice placed their hands strategically on my lower back and hips, using counter-pressure to aid in pain relief. In between the contractions I rested, lying on my side or sitting back. Sometimes we chatted and joked, but mostly things were quiet.

Around ten thirty, our friend Jenny arrived. Though a registered nurse, Jenny had never seen an intervention-free birth, and I had invited her to watch and also act as photographer for the event. Armed with a camera and a rosary, she found a spot in the background where she could pray and take pictures while remaining out of the way.

The whole night felt special. There was something in the air, a powerful sense of peace and beauty that made me feel like I was on the cusp of something great. After all of the affirmation Travis and I had received throughout the pregnancy — after all the ways God had shown us his faithfulness and generosity — I was sure that the baby I was about to deliver had a special life ahead of him.

Bernice checked the baby's heart sounds again, and they were perfect. The transitional phase of labor began, and I remembered the penance given to me when I had gone to confession a few days before: to pray out loud with each contraction, thanking Jesus for my baby and for the experience. I started praying. The contractions were close together now, very long and very strong, and I had to lean on my husband for support. At the beginning and the end of each one, I grunted out a prayer. "Thank you, Jesus."

"Oh, sweet Jesus." "Glory be to God." And because I was in pain, I sometimes included, "Help me, God!" and "Oh, Mother Mary!" The prayers added to the peaceful yet powerful feeling in the air: Something amazing was about to happen.

Travis and I were kneeling on the floor, facing each other, and he was physically supporting me. With my hands pushing onto the tops of his thighs, I pressed my head into his chest as I worked through the contractions. He quietly whispered words of encouragement into my ears, while Kim and Bernice softly commented on how well things were progressing. Knowing the baby was coming soon, Bernice asked Kim for the Doppler to check heart tones. Just as Kim brought it to me, a strong contraction began, and I told them that the baby was coming. They quickly set the Doppler aside and prepared to catch a newborn.

For a moment, caught between the rock and the hard place of push out a baby or stay pregnant forever, I panicked and, like many women before me, said, "I can't do this." Travis told me, "Yes, you can. You've done it before, and you can do this now." Kim, in her best doula voice, told me firmly: "Bonnie, you've got to get this baby out now. You can do this." Slowly, I pushed my baby down, allowing my body time to do what it was supposed to do — to stretch and gently make room. During those last moments, I felt like I was in control: A contraction would come, and I would slowly and carefully push my crowning child out. I knew I was moments away from holding my baby. I knew that very soon I would be showered and wearing fresh pajamas, tucked into bed, and studying the old-man-like face of my newborn. Travis was certain the baby was a boy, and we were moments away from seeing whether he was correct.

One last push, and the head was out. As Bernice guided the body, I gave two more pushes, and my baby boy was born. Bernice swooped him up and placed him into my arms. I was exhausted and needed to sit after hours of kneeling. "Say his name, Bonnie. Say it and rub his back," she commanded me. Bernice sounded urgent, but I was too tired to really notice the tone in her voice. I slowly and gently rubbed his back and dreamily said: "James. Hello, James. It's your mama."

But his arms dangled at his sides. He wasn't crying or moving or breathing, and instead of being a gooey-covered pink, he was ashen blue.

CHAPTER 7

Emergency Baptism

I held him for a moment, and then Bernice took him. Moving swiftly, she placed James on the floor, grabbed her stethoscope, and, with Kim, checked all over his body for a pulse. They couldn't find one. They listened for a heartbeat. Nothing. They spoke urgently and quietly to one another.

Travis sat back on his heels and watched. Jenny shifted back and forth and asked what she could do to help. Kim tried to seal an oxygen mask on James's face, but my ten-pound baby was too big for the newborn mask. Babies sometimes take a moment to breathe after being born; because James's umbilical cord had not yet been cut, there was reasonable hope that he was still receiving oxygen-rich blood, and that all would be well in a moment.

We didn't know, however, that there was a tightly tied true knot in James's umbilical cord. At some point during the twenty minutes of pushing, as James descended the birth canal, that knot tightened, cutting off his supply of oxygen. Born at 1:48

on a Thursday morning, James Fulton was 21.5 inches long and weighed approximately ten pounds. With absolutely no signs of life and an APGAR score of 0, James was stillborn.

As they continued to work on him, he remained lifeless. All my feelings of control and great possibilities rushed out of my chest like water from a broken dam. My baby was dead. I didn't know what was happening, and I didn't understand: He was supposed to have a future filled with hope. But now none of our dreams for him were possible, because he was dead, right in front of me.

In that moment, I had no concrete thoughts, just feelings. I didn't know what was happening and what it all meant, but it felt as if I sat at a great distance from my child and that I was slipping farther and farther away.

Months later, Travis and I walked back through what had happened. I pointed out the spot on the floor where I thought I had been and the spot where I thought James had been. There were yards between the locations. Travis reminded me that at the time, James and I had still been attached to one another by his umbilical cord. James had been only a foot away from me, but to me, in those difficult moments, he seemed completely out of reach.

Sitting on the floor as Bernice and Kim worked on James, I felt removed from the situation, exhausted, and confused. I was shutting down emotionally, going into a state of shock, and everything seemed so slow. I didn't cry. I watched, silently, and if I did shift my body, I did so languidly, as if each limb were heavy and tired.

While Kim and Bernice tried to revive James, Travis looked around the room for water. Taking the cup I had been sipping from throughout labor, he dipped in his fingers and thumb. The water sprinkled down on James's forehead, and with his thumb Travis traced the Sign of the Cross above our son's brow. His voice was soft but clear, even though it was suppressing a great deal of emotion.

"James Fulton, I baptize you in the name of the Father, and of the Son, and of the Holy Spirit."

Everyone in the room whispered, "Amen."

It was the first time that either of us had spoken James's full name. There was power in it, because we had made an intentional decision that every time our children's names are spoken, it will be an invocation of the saints for whom they are named. Jenny later told me that when she heard the name, she was given a vision of St. Mary's Cathedral on Fulton Sheen's ordination day. In those moments she felt God's profound presence, peace, and holiness as she gazed at the altar and an image of Our Lord in Mary's hands. As she felt the power of our Eucharistic Lord, she cried out in her head, "This baby can't die — he's named after a saint!"

I sat on our bedroom floor, watching my husband in what was a truly sorrowful event, yet I was aware of being glad that it was happening. In spite of my confusion, I thought to myself: "This is good. At least we can do this." In times of emergency, the Catholic Church teaches that anyone can validly baptize another, needing only to use water while saying the words, "I baptize you in the name of the Father, and of the Son, and of the Holy Spirit."* I didn't know whether James was truly dead or not, but I was grateful that Christ and our Church had given us the Sacrament of Baptism. When there was nothing else we could do, we could do this. I knew that no matter what happened, we had done all that we could to fulfill our roles as parents — we had been open to life, we had discerned God's will, and we had baptized our son. If the goal of every parent is to get their children to heaven, then at least we would be successful with James.

Meanwhile, Bernice and Kim continued chest compressions and mouth-to-mouth resuscitation on James. Travis sat and watched, his face still and somber, and his eyes filled with sorrow. I looked around the room and tried to take in what was happening and what it meant, but I couldn't. I sat on my bedroom floor, just like in my dream, and I looked at my stillborn son. There were no thoughts racing through my mind, no ideas, just two words. Over and over again, I repeated Fulton Sheen's name.

Scripture tells us, "Likewise the Spirit helps us in our weakness; for we do not know how to pray as we ought, but the Spirit himself intercedes for us with sighs too deep for words" (Rom 8:26). In those moments, I could not pray anything coherent. But for months I had been building up a trusted friendship

---

* See 1983 Code of Canon Law, canon 861 §2.

and establishing the habit of calling on Sheen to pray for my child. As I repeated Fulton Sheen's name, I knew that he and God knew what was needed. While placing James in the Father's hands, I was also placing the responsibility for continued prayerful intercession in Sheen's hands.

CHAPTER 8

"Please Send Life Flight"

Scant minutes had passed, but everything seemed to be happening in slow motion. Jenny, realizing that James was not just a baby who needed a moment to respond, decided to call 911. Jenny, a former pediatric intensive care unit nurse, knew what needed to be said and done. She ran downstairs and told my mother-in-law and Katie (who were sitting in the living room and growing more and more nervous because of the silence from upstairs) to pray.

"Pray. We need you to pray. He's not responding," she told them. Then she picked up a piece of mail from our dining room table and walked out the front door. On the front porch, Jenny read our address off the letter to the dispatcher. "I have a baby, just born, nonresponsive. We are doing CPR. Please send Life Flight. This baby needs to get there fast — can you get me Life Flight?"

The dispatcher promised to do her best, but cautioned Jenny

that there might not be the airspace needed for the helicopter. Hanging up the phone, Jenny went back to the living room and asked my friend Katie to watch for the ambulance. She then returned to the bedroom, and we all waited for the first responders while Bernice and Kim continued CPR. James was still silent, blue, and motionless. There was still no pulse.

The night, which had begun so quietly and beautifully, began to get busier and louder.

The first to arrive at the house were our town's volunteer first responders. Men I had passed on the streets and sidewalks of my small town filled my room. They wore boots and jeans, which they had hastily thrown on as they responded to the call. I didn't know any of them, but I sat before all of them wearing a white tank top, blood, and nothing else. My usually modest self was too tired and too bewildered to care.

They tried to seal the oxygen mask on James's face, but found him to be too big. They checked his body for a pulse, but found none. The paramedics arrived, and Jenny asked them to intubate James — to insert a tube down his throat to deliver oxygen. The lead paramedic explained that they didn't have the equipment, and then cut James's umbilical cord. It was 2:07 in the morning, nineteen minutes after James had been born. Throughout it all, a first responder knelt behind me, supporting me and holding my hand. It was a small gesture, but one so full of compassion that, years later, the memory still makes me cry.

With James finally separated from me, they wrapped him up in a blanket and carried him away. Travis followed so he could ride in the ambulance with our son. As he walked past his mother on the way out of the house, he looked at her and said, "Pray." Travis got in the ambulance, Jenny got in her car, and they all began the drive to OSF Saint Francis Medical Center in downtown Peoria.

Upstairs, I was still on the bedroom floor. Bernice and Kim had been doing their best to monitor me while they worked on James, but now they turned their full attention to me. They asked the last lingering volunteers to give me some privacy, and then helped me with the afterbirth. Amazingly, I hadn't torn at all and didn't need any stitches. Gently but quickly they cleaned me up, helped me into my robe, and prepared me for transfer by ambulance to St. Francis. I asked if I could ride in a car, but an ambulance would get me to my son more quickly, they said. It would also allow for monitoring, something I needed following the traumatic birth. Bernice and Kim reassured me that they would clean up from the delivery and meet me at the hospital.

The volunteer first responders strapped me into a special chair and carried me down the stairs. As I passed my friend and mother-in-law, I didn't speak; I couldn't speak. I just looked at their sorrowful, worried faces and saw that they didn't blame me for what was happening. That was enough.

The first responders carried me through my front yard, which was filled with a surprising number of police and EMTs. Ambulances, police cars, and even a fire truck lined the road. They had come from my town and two surrounding communities. As the red and blue lights lit up the street and houses, I wondered whether my neighbors had any idea what was going on. When I was in the ambulance and on the way to the hospital, the EMTs caring for me told me of their prayers. "As soon as I heard the call come over the radio, my wife and I began to pray for your little boy," one said. "My wife is at home, still praying." I nodded my thanks. I was in shock and could find no words. I needed the prayers of others — strangers, friends, family, and Sheen — to carry me through this moment.

CHAPTER 9

Pulseless Electrical Activity

Meanwhile, the paramedics hooked James to a heart monitor as the ambulance sped toward the hospital. There were no normal spikes to indicate a heartbeat, just sporadic squiggles. The monitor showed "pulseless electrical activity," commonly known as PEA. James's heart was sending out random electrical pulses, but it was not pumping. Legally, he could have been declared dead.

As Travis willed the ambulance to go faster, the paramedics gave James two doses of epinephrine, a drug that can help restart the heart, en route. In hopes that the marrow would quickly absorb the drug, they shot it straight into his shin bones, first on the right leg and then, a few minutes later, the left. Neither worked. And then, because the line into his right tibia was not stable, the drug leaked out, causing a massive chemical burn.

Forty-four minutes after he'd been born, the ambulance arrived at the hospital. The EMTs pulled James's gurney from the ambulance, and Travis watched as one of the medics knelt over James, continuing the chest compressions as the gurney was rolled toward the awaiting emergency department team. Standing with the doctors and nurses were two nurse practitioners from the neonatal intensive care unit (NICU). One look at the baby, and they knew he was dead. His coloring was somewhere between gray and white, and except for moving with the force of the chest compressions, he was completely motionless. They wheeled James into a room, and Travis followed. He didn't know what to do or where to stand, but he wanted to be close.

Inside the emergency room, everyone went to work. A nurse searched James's body for a pulse, checking every possible location, but found none. Technicians hooked James up to monitors, but he continued to register as PEA. The NICU nurse practitioners intubated him. Chest compressions continued. They administered more epinephrine. As they worked, they also spoke with the on-call neonatologist, Dr. Corrales. They told her that he was not responding to the medicine. She told them to try for a bit longer and then declare time of death.

Because no one could feel a pulse or hear a heartbeat with a stethoscope, they brought in a sonogram machine so they could see, via ultrasound on a computer screen, what the baby's heart was doing. The room was even more crowded now, so Travis stepped out. In the hall he met Jenny. He looked her in the eyes and said, "I guess heaven is better, right?" The two stood outside the door and prayed.

Inside the room, the doctor looked at James's heart on the

screen; it sat still. They administered more epinephrine and followed that with another sonogram.

"The heart just fluttered," the doctor said.

"You mean like a beat?" a hopeful nurse asked.

"No. Just a flutter."

The team reported the new movement — an ineffective, unorganized heartbeat — to the neonatologist, who encouraged them to keep trying. If nothing else happened in that time, the head emergency department doctor was to call time of death. It had now been fifty-one minutes since James's birth.

A nurse held on to James's little foot, wanting to comfort the unresponsive baby. He was cold, she later said, calling to her mind the expression "cold and dead." Everyone in the room knew that things didn't look good, and that the flutter of a heartbeat didn't bring hope.

As each second passed and became another minute without a heartbeat, they knew that even if James came back to life, it would not be good. The human body needs oxygen, and even the best CPR cannot suffice indefinitely. If James's heart restarted, the damage to his organs from a lack of oxygen would be severe and most likely fatal. A nurse checked the clock and began to worry about the balance of the greater good: life vs. quality of life. With that consideration, one of the NICU nurse practitioners spoke on the phone with Dr. Corrales.

"We've been working on him for eighteen minutes, and there's nothing. What do you want us to do?"

Dr. Corrales replied, "Try for just a bit longer and then call it." It had now been fifty-six minutes.

She was following protocol. Babies are remarkably resilient, but Dr. Corrales knew that after twelve minutes, there was little hope. In fact, many doctors would have just called time of death right then. A few more minutes would not bring back our son, but it would allow the doctors to tell Travis that they had done everything they could.

And so they continued chest compressions, watched the monitors, and did everything else within their power to bring James back to life. Later, we learned that at this point the goal was not to save his life; everyone knew that even if his heart began to beat again, he would not live for long. The goal was for James to have a pulse long enough for his parents to hold a warm, living baby, tell him they loved him, and say goodbye.

In the end, though, James was still motionless and cold. At 2:49 in the morning, after the window of time had closed for any resuscitating drugs to work, the doctors and nurses stopped. They took their hands off James — who by now had been without a pulse for sixty-one minutes — and prepared to call his time of death.

At that moment, astonishingly, James's heart began to beat.

It spontaneously shot up to a healthy 148 beats per minute, and it never stopped again.

CHAPTER 10

Keep Faith

When James came back to life, the emergency department staff jumped into action. Because his veins were so little, a surgeon had to insert a line into an artery near his leg. He was given fluids and sedation drugs; and, because he had a small seizure, he was also given phenobarbital to stop any further episodes.

At this point the doctors — four men with tears in their eyes — came out of the room and stood before Travis and Jenny. "Are you James's dad?" the lead doctor asked.

Travis nodded. The doctor continued: "Your son is alive, and they're transferring him to the NICU. He didn't have a pulse when he came in, and he didn't have one for a long time, but he has a one now. We did all that we could."

Sorrow, compassion, and regret filled the faces of the emergency department staff. Later, we learned that it was because many of them wondered, "What have we done?" Yes, James was unexpectedly, shockingly alive, but they knew that his life would most likely be short and horrible. Many of the nurses and doctors felt that it would have been better if he had never revived.

When James stabilized, the nurse practitioners began his quick transport and transfer to the NICU just a few floors above at the Children's Hospital of Illinois. Travis and Jenny accompanied James and the nurses as they hustled through the maze of pristine tunnels and elevators.

Recognizing one of the nurse practitioners, Jenny moved over to her. "Julie, it's Jenny. You taught me while I was in nursing school." Julie immediately recognized Jenny, and they spoke briefly about what had happened.

"What are his blood pH levels?" Jenny asked.

"6.7," Julie said. Both knew too well that anything less than 7.0 means the blood has turned acidic, and death has begun to take over the body. James may have been alive in that moment, but he would certainly not remain so for long.

Meanwhile, I was on the labor and delivery floor in another part of the hospital. The doctors and nurses wanted to give me Pitocin to control postpartum bleeding, but as they bustled around me I kept saying that I was fine, that I didn't want Pitocin, but I could use some ibuprofen. "Just give me some pain medicine and let me go see my son."

Travis, who had been joined by the hospital chaplain, came to my room. He looked completely exhausted, and with tears in his eyes he stood by my bed, touched my arm, and said with complete sincerity: "He's alive. Keep faith. He's going to be fine." He was convinced, and with a peace that surpassed all understanding he knew in his heart that James would be okay.

I heard his words, but they meant very little to me. I knew nothing of what had happened after James was carried out of our bedroom, but the tears in Travis's eyes seemed to communicate that the situation was bad. I was confused by his confidence and wondered why he felt the need to tell me these things. Yet, in the back of my mind, I was operating under the vague thought that of course James would be fine. He was at the hospital, and they would save him.

I took Travis's hand. "Okay," I said, and then turned to the nurses and doctors and asked to go see my son. Again, they tried to give me Pitocin, and again I told them I didn't want it. I noticed that the chaplain was still standing in the doorway, his Roman collar slightly crooked and his dark, curly hair disheveled. He was speaking with a nurse, and I assumed that he was asking her to let me leave for the NICU. Meanwhile, Travis firmly told the doctor that we would not use the Pitocin, and he asked for a wheelchair. The doctor compromised and offered to let me leave the floor as long as a nurse with a shot of Pitocin in her pocket could accompany me. With everything arranged and me sitting in a wheelchair, Travis finally introduced me to Monsignor Michael Bliss, the chaplain, and pushed me to the NICU.

When we arrived at James's room, we found him lying in a small bed, surrounded by medical equipment and people in scrubs. He looked so vulnerable, but we trusted that the medical team was taking good care of him. In those moments, Travis and I didn't know what was really happening. We were operating mostly on muscle memory and whatever emotions penetrated our shock. We weren't considering biology and basic medical science. We definitely weren't adding up minutes or thinking about brain damage and organ failure. But that was what everyone else was doing.

CHAPTER 11

Confirmation

Shortly after our arrival at the NICU, Father Donton arrived. Jenny had called him, waking him in the middle of the night. He spoke with Monsignor Bliss, and the two approached Travis and me. Their clothes were slightly tousled, and they looked a little wild-eyed; noticing their appearances, I glanced around at the rest of us. The nurses all had their hair done and makeup on; they were wide awake and going about their normal routine. Those in our group, though, were exhausted and running on adrenaline. Physically and emotionally, we were ragged; personally, I was weak.

"How are you, Bonnie?" Father Donton asked.

"I'm okay. I'm in a lot of pain."

"I'm sure." He put his hand on my shoulder and continued in a gentle voice. "Monsignor Bliss has offered to confirm James if you and Travis would like that."

I looked at Travis. This wasn't a decision I thought we'd be asked to make. On one level I was aware that the Latin rite Catholic Church only confirms little ones when they are going to die.[*] I knew that this suggestion came with great compassion, offering us an opportunity to ensure James had all the graces needed to suffer and die a holy death. Confirmation would make him a full member of the Catholic Church, something that was deeply important to Travis and me. We also knew that, like the emergency baptism, this was a chance for us to parent James when there was nothing else we could do. If our primary goal as parents is to get our children to heaven, we knew that the priests before us were offering to help us make that happen as beautifully, peacefully, and gracefully as possible. On one level I knew all this.

But mostly I was operating in a state of shock, pain, and disbelief, so I responded with my first thought: "What will happen when he's in eighth grade and all his friends are being confirmed?"

Father Donton and Monsignor Bliss looked at each other. I could sense that they understood something to which I was oblivious; but with great patience and consideration, Monsignor answered me. "Well, if that happens, he will take the class and go through all the preparation with his classmates, but he just won't be a part of the Mass when everyone else is confirmed. He'll probably be an altar server."

Travis looked at me again and said, "Well, why wouldn't we?"

"Yeah, let's do it then," I answered.

---

* See 1983 Code of Canon Law, canons 883 3°, 889 §2, and 891.

The nurses and technicians made room so that Travis and I and the priests could be next to the crib. Travis pushed my wheelchair next to James, and I reached out to touch him for the first time since I had held him after his birth.

"You can touch his hands and feet, but you can't hold your hand on his head or body, because it will warm him up," a nurse explained to me.

"He's shivering. He's cold," I said.

They explained that James was undergoing cooling therapy. The blue pad he was lying on lowered his body temperature by a few degrees, and the lower temperature helped prevent further and ongoing damage to his organs. If he was warm, it wouldn't work.

"It's like Han Solo in *Star Wars*?" I asked.

Travis and the nurse smiled at me. "Yes, it's kinda like Han Solo." She then pointed out all the tubes and wires and patches on James, explaining what each one did. A feeding tube, a breathing tube, and an internal thermometer were all down his throat. There were IVs into the large veins near his groin and his umbilical cord vessels. There were wires on his chest, foot, and finger to monitor his oxygen levels, heart rate, and other vital signs. He was heavily sedated, and the ventilator breathed for him. He didn't move except for an occasional shiver.

I noticed that his right leg was purple, blue, and black and asked what had happened. They explained that the epinephrine had leaked out during the ambulance ride. I studied my baby boy, his face, his fingers, his toes, his chest. Except for his leg, his body was now a healthy, ruddy pink, but covered in all those wires and tubes and surrounded by the sounds of the beeping monitors, whooshing ventilator, and whispering nurses, he seemed so, so sick. To me, he looked much worse in that NICU bed alive than he had appeared when lifeless and cradled in my arms. I was scared.

"Travis and Bonnie, we're ready," Monsignor said. "Everyone, we're going to confirm James now. Please pray with us."

The nurses stepped back from James, and my mother-in-law, Bernice, Kim, and Jenny — who had all since arrived and had been waiting in the hallway — stepped into the room or stood in the doorway. Monsignor stood by James's head at the end of the crib, with Father Donton at his side. Travis and I stayed at the side of the crib as Monsignor began to speak.

"Do you have a confirmation name you'd like to use?"

Without hesitation, I raised my hand and definitively shouted, "Linus." Seizing the opportunity to use the name I had wanted, I spoke before Travis could even open his mouth. Everyone chuckled, and the ceremony began. The fragrant chrism glistened on James Fulton Linus's forehead. Everyone in the room prayed the Our Father. I held his little hand; Travis touched his little foot.

As the ceremony ended, the nurses came back to his crib, and everyone went back to the hallway except for Travis and me. I felt like I had fully surrendered my son. He was God's, and God was in control.

CHAPTER 12

A Grim Outlook

Shortly after the confirmation, I asked to be taken home. I needed to sleep and wanted to shower and to see my other children. Travis stayed with James while Bernice and Kim drove me back to my house. On the road, I noticed that it was a little after six in the morning. I pointed out the time and said: "We were supposed to call my mom at six and give her an update. I don't think I will. I don't think I can." My voice faded, and there was a long pause in the van as I thought. I didn't want to break the news to anyone. I didn't want to tell the story or answer questions. I didn't want people to tell me, "I'm sorry," and I didn't want to hear sadness in their voices. I felt a stupid responsibility to comfort people, to tell them that everything would be okay, that James would be okay, to make them happy. I didn't have the energy to do this, but I also didn't know what else to do. I wanted to avoid the situation completely.

Kim broke the silence. "Bonnie, why don't you want to

tell your mom?"

I stared out the window. "I don't want to make her sad."

"She'll want to know."

"You can call and tell her. Would you call her and tell her?"

Bernice turned her eyes from the road for a moment to look at me and gently said, "I think she'll want to hear from you."

Kim leaned toward me and said: "As a mom, I would want to hear from my daughter. She'll want to support you, Bonnie. You should tell her. You can use my phone."

Kim passed her phone to me, and I punched in my parents' number. Mom answered with a bright, expectant voice. I told her the details, asked her to phone family, and told her that yes, I would really like it if she came over to the house.

Calling my mom was the best thing I could have done. Her voice was full of comfort and hope.

At home, I eased up the stairs to my front door. My friend Katie was taking care of Lydia and Bennet, and they all greeted me with a hug. Because I was too weak for any more stairs, Bernice and Kim made a bed for me on my sofa. I took some ibuprofen and lay down to sleep. Katie sat by me and supported me through the afterpains. I was exhausted, still in shock, and relieved when I felt myself drifting away.

Several hours later, I woke up feeling much better. The first thing I did was ask for a piece of peanut butter toast with Craisins. Then I hobbled to the computer and pulled up my blog. My friends and family knew that I had gone into labor the night before. I knew they were praying for me, and almost twenty-four hours later they would be worried. I also knew that James would need much more prayer.

I typed a post for my blog and shared the link on Facebook. I gave them the details: time of birth, name, weight, and length. I briefly described the traumatic birth and explained that he was in critical condition at the NICU.

I noted the possibility that James would suffer brain and organ damage, thanked the many people who had helped us so far, and closed with a plea:

> And now we ask that you will pray for our son. Please pray through the intercession of Saint James, Saint Linus, and Archbishop Sheen. If James comes through with no problems, we will definitely attribute it to a miracle for our local saint.

> PLEASE PRAY!

We needed every prayer we could get.

James had been born in the early morning on a Thursday, and the doctors and nurses caring for him didn't know if he would live through his birthday. Maybe he would live through the weekend. Most would have agreed he wouldn't live through the week, and several of the nurses expected to see his crib empty when they returned for their next shift the following weekend. Some of our friends and family looked at their calendars and wondered when the funeral would be and what they would need to shift in their schedules to attend it.

As the doctors studied James's medical records from my midwife and the emergency room, they added up the time from his birth to when his heart began to beat again. James's primary doctor looked at the notations again and again.

"That's not right," she said. "That can't be right." She looked at Travis and me and asked us what time James had been born. Then she looked back at the medical records on the computer screen.

Sixty-one minutes was too long to be without a heartbeat and then come back to life.

She decided to walk down to the emergency department to discuss James's arrival with the staff. They confirmed everything: He had been born at 1:48 in the morning, reportedly without a pulse. He had arrived at the emergency department PEA. Nurses had looked all over his body for a pulse and could find none, and he continued to be PEA on the monitor throughout his time in the emergency room, a total of seventeen minutes. Despite her disbelief, it was a fact: James had been dead for more than an hour. She ordered EEGs and MRIs to assess the situation we were facing.

The first EEG — a test that measures the electrical activity of the brain — took place while James was still sedated and undergoing cooling therapy. It showed only that James was sedated. The second EEG took place shortly after the cooling therapy ended, when he was three days old. The report from the second test was devastating: James's brain was highly abnormal.

His MRI, a scan of brain tissue, also showed injury to the brain, attributed to severe hypoxic ischemia — his brain had been severely deprived of oxygen.

Armed with this information, the hospital staff knew what James's future entailed. They always tried to give us hope — no one wants to take away a parent's hope — but really, they were waiting for the inevitable. All of his organs would begin slowly shutting down, one by one, until he was dead. When they said, "We don't know — he may be fine," it was obvious that they didn't believe it.

So when he did not die within the first few days, they expected him to be in a vegetative state for his very short life. If, for some astounding reason, he improved beyond that point, the prognosis was that he would be severely disabled.

As a parade of experts came through and discussed James's future with us, we slowly got a more detailed picture of what he — and we — faced. His physical therapist explained that cerebral palsy would seriously impact James's body. His muscles would be tight, and his body would be permanently folded in upon itself. His thumbs would be locked against the palms of his hands, which would likely continually be in a fist. His elbows would be bent, most likely with his arms always against his chest. His legs, too, would be locked into some sort of bent, possibly contorted, position. We would have to massage his muscles daily, to bring him comfort and relief. Not only would we never see him walk, but the odds were that he would never be able to hold our hands or wrap his arms around us.

The developmental pediatrician, a specialist with Easter-seals, warned that James would probably be unable to control his body and would need to be strapped into a wheelchair once he was older. Mentally, he would never develop beyond the level of an infant or toddler. He would most likely be blind and unable to talk, suffer from seizures, and be in diapers for the rest of his life.

Some days later, when James had been weaned off most of his support, his feeding and speech therapist sat down with me in our NICU room. James wasn't taking his bottle well, she said, and a test showed he was silently aspirating food into his lungs. His lungs could easily be filling with liquid, but because he didn't cough — which would help clear them — we would never know. She further explained that his gag reflex was inconsistent and that he needed his feedings through a feeding tube.

I asked her whether she thought James would ever overcome these things to eat and drink normally, explaining that I want-ed him to be a part of the family: eating homemade pizza while watching Bears football games, having cake at his first birthday party, enjoying family dinners and celebrations.

"Probably not," she told me. This broke my heart. As she sat on the stool with her blond hair in a perky ponytail and her crossed legs balancing paperwork, she wanted to give me a chance to hope; but instead, she took away my last piece of normal. For some reason I could handle having a son in a wheelchair who couldn't see or speak. But I always imagined that even if we had to feed him and hold the cup to his mouth, he would still be able to eat and drink.

For the first time, I understood what people meant when they talked about quality of life. I struggled with feelings of anger over the pro-life rhetoric that I had always believed.

The pro-life community tells us that every person has dignity, is made in the image and likeness of God, is beautiful. As a part of that community, I had always believed these things. I agreed that even those who seem to have lesser lives, because they can't do the same things that everyone else can, do still lead lives filled with beauty, joy, love, and goodness. I recognized that people with disabilities can teach the rest of us many important lessons.

But as these experts gave me their opinions about my own son, I felt that I no longer believed any of it. I didn't want my son to be someone else's lesson — I wanted my son to lead a normal life. Even in those dark moments I suspected that in the future I would understand much more fully how precious my son's life was, even if he did struggle with cerebral palsy and other difficulties. I knew in a dim way that the truth of the value of his life would become part of my testimony. But in those hours and days and weeks, learning what probably lay ahead for my son just smacked me in the face and ripped out of my hands all the hopes and dreams I had for him, my family, and myself.

Travis and I grieved the son we thought we were going to have, and we grieved the life we thought he would have. We grieved the future we had envisioned for ourselves and our other children. During the pregnancy, we believed with such certainty that this baby was a great gift from God. But now we wondered whether we had somehow gotten in God's way, manipulating our son back to life through modern medicine.

We wondered, especially in light of my dream about a stillborn son, whether God's will had been for us to just accept the death of our son at his birth. We wondered whether we should have not called 911, but instead just held him and planned a funeral.

In spite of everything, though, we continued to pray for a miraculous, full restoration, calling on the intercession of Fulton Sheen. We believed that if God wanted to perform a miracle, he could and would. At the same time, we had no idea what God's plan was, but knew we had to accept whatever God wanted for James — and for us. If that meant James would have severe disabilities, then so be it.

We weren't sure what God was doing or planning to do, but we wanted to make sure that, while remaining persistent in our prayer, we also stood out of God's way. With all that in mind, we asked for a DNR (do not resuscitate) order. This was not because we had given up hope or wanted an easy out. We asked for the DNR because we trusted in God, and we also felt that James had been through enough. If our son crashed now, we didn't want him to have to relive all the tubes and drugs and trauma. He was baptized and confirmed, and we concluded that if God let him crash, then we would let him go to heaven.

CHAPTER 13

Praying for a Miracle

The Saturday morning after James's birth, Travis and I woke up early and put on our Sunday best.

My mother-in-law was staying with us, and together we dressed Lydia and Bennet in their church clothes, ate breakfast, and headed to the hospital. Already the way to the NICU was becoming familiar. This exit, then this turn, drop off the car for the free valet parking, awkwardly manage the huge revolving door, then up the escalator to the third floor.

My parents were already there in the NICU waiting area. Because Lydia and Bennet were so young, they were not allowed to visit James. Two-year-old Lydia would have behaved herself, but curious, one-year-old Bennet surely would have unplugged a monitor or knocked over a machine. They stayed with my dad in the kid-friendly waiting room while Deb, my mom, Travis, and I swiped our ID cards, scrubbed our hands and arms for three minutes, and headed back to James's room.

We were only at the hospital for a brief visit before heading to a holy hour and Mass being held on our son's behalf just blocks away, at the Cathedral of Saint Mary of the Immaculate Conception. Jenny and Katie had planned the event, specifically arranging that it take place in the same cathedral where Archbishop Sheen had served Mass as a boy and been ordained a priest as a young man. We would all pray before God, but would ask Fulton Sheen for his intercession, too. We had stopped by the hospital to collect the latest news on James so we could share it with our friends and family at the cathedral.

We waited for James's primary doctor and the rest of the team to gather in James's room for their morning rounds. By the third day in the NICU, we already knew that we'd get the best information and updates during rounds when James's primary doctor, his nurses, nurse practitioners, and other members of his medical team reviewed his previous twenty-four hours, and discussed his care going forward.

After twenty-five minutes passed, we asked James's nurse if she knew when the doctor would arrive, explaining that we had a prayer service beginning in thirty-five minutes. She looked at the clock and said: "They're still in their morning meeting, but I can ask them if they'll start soon — and I'll explain about the prayer service. They'll come here first because they always start with the sickest baby on the floor."

As soon as the last words left her mouth, I could see by the expression on her face that she regretted it.

"I have the sickest baby in the NICU?" I asked. Travis and

Mom looked at me with compassion as I realized the weight of what she said. OSF is a magnet hospital, drawing patients from throughout Illinois, and it has the only level three NICU in the region outside of Chicago and St. Louis. In the hospital for the sickest babies, on the floor for the sickest babies, my baby was the sickest. I probably should have realized this, but I hadn't. The information momentarily knocked the wind out my sails, but I appreciated the perspective.

Minutes later, the doctor arrived with her team, and the conversation began. Discussions during rounds always happened the exact same way. The medical team would talk about by James using words, numbers, and abbreviations that I did not understand. During this part we sat silently, me with my black-and-white Mead notebook open, jotting down notes and jargon. During the second part, the lead doctor would use laymen's terms to explain to us what the group had just discussed. I would continue to take notes, writing down numbers and doing my best to spell out medical words phonetically. Last, we would ask questions, and team members would provide definitions, make clarifications, and sometimes draw diagrams on pieces of paper towel. That day, the bottom line was that soon they'd slowly warm James up and take him off the cooling therapy, and it was essential that the process go well.

With our update complete, we kissed James and made the Sign of the Cross on his forehead. We watched him shiver, told him we loved him, and promised we'd return later. Then we headed back to the waiting room, the elevator, and the valet, climbed in our cars, and drove to the cathedral.

Archbishop Sheen once wrote, "You will have to fight many battles, but do not worry, because in the end you will win the war before the Blessed Sacrament."* With that truth lodged in our hearts, we climbed the stone stairs that led to the massive front doors of St. Mary's. As we stepped into the narthex, we saw Jenny and some other friends standing by a table with black-and-white pictures of James and a stack of cards printed with the prayer to obtain a favor through the intercession of Archbishop Sheen. The prayer specifically asked that James's body heal and function normally, and that he be spared any brain damage.

We each picked up a prayer card, and Travis and I bent down to point out the pictures of James to Lydia and Bennet. They knew they had a brother but had not yet met him, and I hoped the pictures would help them connect with and care for him.

My parents and Deb made their way into the church, but Travis and I stayed in the back a little while longer, peering through the windows and taking everything in. There were easily more than one hundred people in the cathedral that morning: my older brother, my grandparents, James's godfather and his family, many friends, people I only recognized but did not personally know, and people who were strangers to Travis and me.

Saint Paul called all Christians the Body of Christ. At times the Church — the Body of Christ — is accused of limping along or, worse yet, sleeping, being inactive, and failing to pay atten-

---

* Fulton J. Sheen, *Treasure of Clay* (San Francisco: Ignatius Press, 2018), 195.

tion. This was not what my family experienced. If the Body of Christ had ever been asleep, then James's birth awoke the giant. It seemed to us that the Church — so often scolded for being stingy, scrupulous, and judgmental — was just waiting for an opportunity to serve and to use her gifts and talents to give back to God. There she was, the Body of Christ, giving up Saturday morning, sitting in the pews, praying for and supporting us.

Travis and I led the kids to the pew where my parents were. The holy hour was half over, but we were grateful for the thirty minutes we still had to kneel before the Eucharist in silence. We didn't have to think or answer questions or speak with people. The church was silent except for the occasional creak of the wooden pews, and I appreciated this little bit of peace in the midst of such a powerful storm.

As Mass began, I was thankful for the familiarity of the liturgy. We said the responses, stood, sat, kneeled, listened, prayed, and sang. The priest who celebrated the Mass urged us to trust in God and not lose hope. He didn't promise a miracle, but he did promise that when it was too hard for Travis and me to hope, they would carry us in hope. He encouraged the Body of Christ to believe, to pray, and to act.

My body was still sore from labor and delivery, and emotionally I was worn out, but as we stood at the end of Mass to recite the prayer for a miracle through the intercession of Fulton Sheen, I wondered what God would do. Jesus had turned water into wine when his mother asked, and had healed the servant when the centurion asked. Now we were asking. Would he say yes to our prayers and Fulton Sheen's prayers and heal my son?

Travis and I went to the pulpit after the time of prayer concluded to give our update about James. I thanked everyone for coming and for supporting us and asked them to continue to pray. Travis described the cooling therapy, and with tears in his eyes told everyone that James would be okay. I was a little bit embarrassed by such a bold statement, but also in awe of my husband's ability to be so bold and to believe so wholeheartedly. I prayed his faith would be rewarded.

In the following days and weeks, the blog post I had written on James's birthday flew around the internet. All over Facebook I saw my friends request prayers for James and our family. Bible studies, moms' groups, and families gathering for nightly prayers interceded for our son. Small children adopted James as their main prayer intention. Church prayer-chain emails asked for prayer. Friends who taught in Catholic schools had their students recite the prayer for a miracle through Fulton Sheen's intercession on a daily basis. Even atheists I knew contacted their Christian friends to suggest they pray for my son.

From New York to California, Alaska to Texas, Germany to Mexico — people all over the world were praying as James's story spread through blogs and Facebook, texts and tweets and emails. I couldn't help but think that Archbishop Sheen — who had used every form of media available to him to evangelize — was loving it. It seemed incredibly appropriate that he was the saint we were relying on.

Chapter 14

Pick Up Your Mat and Walk

Meanwhile, it wasn't always easy to figure out what was going on with James.

While it was incredible that he came back to life after being dead for an hour, we still didn't know what kind of life he had been brought back to, though all realistic possibilities seemed grim. If there was a miracle unfolding, it was hard to see.

In the gospels, Jesus healed people instantly, and it was instantly obvious. He told the crippled man, "Rise, take up your pallet, and walk" (Jn 5:8), and the man did, after being unable to walk for thirty-eight years. Our slowly unfolding miracle, if it was a miracle, wasn't like that. James couldn't pick up his mat. He was a newborn who couldn't even lift his head. Added to his natural limitations because of his age was the fact that he had been sedated throughout his NICU stay, so when there were issues, setbacks, or concerns, there was always the question of whether it was because of the medicine or because of the lack of oxygen at birth.

Because he was still undergoing cooling therapy, I was unable to hold my son, who continued to shiver as he lay uncovered in an open-air crib. I would stand next to him and study his wire-covered body. He looked so frail, and I felt broken as I studied his eyes. His pupils did not dilate. His eyes did not focus on anything. When the nurse moved her hand close to his eyes, he did not blink. We didn't know whether this meant he was blind, severely brain damaged, or simply on a lot of medications. The spectrum of possibilities was almost unbearable.

In response to all the unknowns, we prayed and shared specific prayer intentions with friends, family, and those who were following the story online. James was just one day old when I wrote on my blog: "Well, we need you to pray for pee for James Fulton. Right now it is very important that his kidneys begin to function better. Once that happens, they can give him more 'good stuff,' including nutrients. Specifically, because he's puffy, we need him to pee 5 ml per-kilo per-hour until he pulls through. Then he'll need to pee 2 ml per-kilo per-hour. I ask you to specifically pray for that. Storm heaven."

Never would I have thought I'd be begging anyone to pray for urine-filled diapers, but there I was with a newborn carrying two extra pounds of water weight, and I was asking not only for pee, but also for a specific amount of fluid ounces and on a timeline. The next day at the hospital, we learned that not only had James peed, but he had peed double the amount they had hoped to see. On top of it all, he had pooped! Blessed, amazing, wonderful poop!

That poopy diaper was a sign of hope. Since a hierarchy exists for our organs, our bodies shut down certain nonessential tasks and even make some organs go into a sort of hibernation mode when the oxygen supply is not sufficient. Once the body has exhausted all its self-preservation tactics, it starts to shut down, beginning with the brain. The NICU staff believed all of James's organs would be gravely damaged from his pulseless sixty-one minutes, yet his intestines were working, along with the more important liver and kidneys. This information gave the doctors and nurses hope that maybe the damage in James's brain would not be as bad as they had suspected.

His diapers clearly showed us that his colon and kidneys were healthy at two days old. At three days, James's doctor told us his heart and lungs were fine. By four days his leg, the one that had suffered a chemical burn from epinephrine and probably would have been amputated because of necrosis, was pink with only two dark spots. In time, those spots would become scabs, and then just scars.

At six days old, James was done with cooling therapy, as well as several of his tubes and wires. This meant I was able to hold him for the first time since his birth. As I sang and talked to him, I noticed that his once-blank eyes were now following me. His eyes changed as people moved and created shadows. As he watched us, we felt certain: If James had been blind, now he could see.

Just three days later, at nine days old, James was breathing room air on his own — something we had feared his injured brain would never let him do.

As the days and weeks passed, we rode the emotional roller coaster of good days and very tough ones. There were setbacks and hard news, but overall it seemed that James was improving, and our prayers were being answered.

Chapter 15

The Day-to-Day

It wasn't long before we had a new routine as a family. Travis would rise while the rest of us slept and leave extra early for work so he could spend time sitting with his son in the NICU every morning. He would leave before the 7:00 a.m. shift change, attending a local parish's Communion service before heading on to work.

I rose with Lydia and Bennet, who were now two and a half and one. We'd have breakfast, get dressed, and play. Block towers were knocked down, board books were read, and trains chugged through the house.

And then the Body of Christ would show up, knocking at our door. Every day people came to help. Often it was my mom, but friends came too, bringing packages with presents for Lydia and Bennet; NICU survival kits of fresh fruit, hand lotion, mints, and bottled water for Travis and me; and special tokens for James. There were meals that came every day for seven weeks. People brought us necessities like bread, toilet paper, cereal, and toothpaste in case we didn't have time to get to the store. Someone mowed our lawn. Someone arranged the schedule so that Travis and I could have a date night. Someone else took over mailing out my thank-you notes to the people who were helping us. They cleaned my house and folded my laundry.

And that wasn't all. Every day people would reassure us of their prayers. Friends, family, and acquaintances mailed or dropped off thoughtful and loving cards, some of which were filled with cash, checks, gas cards, or gift cards to local restaurants.

We had worried about what people would think of us — did they blame us because we had chosen a homebirth? But instead of judgment, we found generosity and care. Their magnanimity allowed us to set aside so many concerns and focus on being present to our children at home and James in the NICU. So often during my pregnancy with James, we had felt that God was taking care of us. Now that we were in the midst of a chaotic and traumatic situation, he continued to provide for us, supporting us through his Mystical Body, the Church.

In the late morning or early afternoon, with friends or family present to babysit my other kids, I would leave for my daily visit with James. I often imagined Fulton Sheen climbing into the van with me. I pictured Saints Elizabeth, James the Greater, Gianna, Joan of Arc, and others filling up the van, with Mary riding shotgun. The twenty-two-minute drive from my home to the NICU felt long and lonely day after day, and I was grateful for the company. In what could have been an excruciatingly painful and isolating time for my family, we were instead bolstered by the faith, hope, and love of so many.

By the end of our first week in the NICU, everything was familiar to me. Valet parking, main entrance, elevators up, swipe my badge, and the whoosh of the doors as they opened for me to enter. I walked straight to the sink, opened a small scrub brush, and began the three-minute process of washing my arms, hands, fingers, and nails. I then headed back to James's room, where a little blue-and-green caterpillar spelled out his name on the door. I'd pull the sleek, blue recliner closer to his crib and try to take everything in. A statue of Our Lady holding the infant Christ and a Fulton Sheen holy card were taped to the side of his crib, keeping watch. Though he was now breathing room air and was done with cooling therapy, there were still so many remaining tubes, wires, and beeping machines, and I was afraid of hurting him further.

Often, I would stand for a long while, gently holding his hand, and singing "My Savior's Love Endures" over him. The song by J. J. Heller, a version of Mary's Magnificat, was my prayer for him and with him, sung to will myself to believe its words while also finding great comfort in them. I spent so much of my days begging God and Fulton Sheen for a miracle; but with this song, there were "no petitions but only praise," as Fulton Sheen himself once wrote.* I sang it over and over again, day after day, week after week. "He has done mighty things; holy is his name," I would sing with tears roll-

---

* Fulton J. Sheen, *The World's First Love*, 2nd ed. (San Francisco: Ignatius Press, 2010), 45.

ing down my cheeks, the lump in my throat occasionally blocking the words.

As nurses and doctors came in to check on James, I would get updates on how he had done in the last twenty-four hours and what the goals were for the day. I would hold him, feed him, and put lip balm on his dry little lips. I studied his body and listened to his breathing. And if he had finally fallen asleep after a long battle, I would leave him alone, reading a book or posting an update as I sat right next to him.

Sometimes I ate at the hospital, but often I'd return home to eat dinner with Travis, Lydia, and Bennet. We would feast on the meal that had been provided for us and then settle down for a couple hours of snuggles and family time before bed. Every night, Travis and I would review the day that had happened and the days that were coming. We clung to each other, figuratively and literally, as we prayed for a miracle and thanked God for his provisions. And then, mentally, emotionally, and physically exhausted, we would fall asleep to do it all again the next day.

CHAPTER 16

A G-Tube and Discharge

The weeks passed, and September turned into October. James seemed to be steadily improving in so many ways, but one of the setbacks we kept encountering was his eating. He had to undergo multiple "cookie swallows," tests where he was x-rayed while drinking bottles of formula thickened to various degrees and mixed with barium. We already knew his gag reflex was poor, but with these tests we watched him aspirate unthickened liquids, if he ate anything.

Throughout each day I begged God to heal James; and as various test dates approached, I doubled down on my prayers, pleading for things to go well. Over the weeks, my prayers morphed from a small, scared, "Please, God, help him" to a desperate, "What is your will, what is your will, what is your will, WHAT IS YOUR WILL?!" That turned into, "Oh, my God, oh, my God, I'm so scared, oh, my God, please heal him, I'm so scared, so please heal him, heal him, heal him, my God, just do this, just do this, please, just heal him!"

Finally, exhausted, scared, and overwhelmed, I prayed: "I confess that I am scared. I have doubts. But I am giving you my doubts and fears, and I am asking you to fill that space with trust. I believe; help my unbelief."

Peace came then, but my battle with fear was not over. James had days where he victoriously chugged bottles, but he didn't consistently eat well, even with milkshake-thick bottles of formula. His feedings were usually finished by a feeding tube that snaked from his nose down to his stomach. As our son fattened up, Travis and I wondered whether he was just not as hungry as the dietician thought he should be; but his feeding therapist labeled him a disorganized eater and was concerned. In the end, Travis and I agreed to the surgical placement of a feeding tube into his stomach, commonly called a g-tube.

I pretended to be brave about the g-tube. I pretended that I could handle it, and I hoped the mantra "fake it till ya make it" actually worked, because once the surgery was done, James came home. He wasn't carrying his own mat yet, but, as one nurse told me with tear-filled eyes, "He just seems like a normal baby now." He was ready for discharge.

For seven weeks, James had been hooked up to monitors that beeped and kept track of his heart rate and oxygen levels. Every diaper he wore was weighed before being thrown away. Every ounce he did or did not consume was noted. Before anyone touched him, they washed or sanitized their hands. His room was cleaned every single day. For seven weeks, he had been cared for by medical professionals, from nurses' assistants to expensive specialists with lots of letters behind their names.

Now he was coming home. At our house, the only monitor was the one at his crib that let me hear him when he woke up for feedings. At our house, there'd be no warning sounds if his heart stopped again, if he had a seizure, or if something else went terribly wrong. At our house, we would not wash our hands before we touched him, and I knew that he would be spending time lying on a floor that was vacuumed only once a week at best. At home, his big brother and sister would sneeze and cough on him, and smother him with sloppy kisses. But worst of all, at home his primary caregiver would be a woman who was intimidated by any bodily messes or issues that were more complicated than a poopy diaper or a cut that could be covered by a Band-Aid.

Poor James had to rely on me to care for him and not freak out when the direct opening to his stomach "sharted" out a puke-smelling, gross mixture of formula, rice cereal, and stomach acid. I did not do well with this, and sometimes we just looked each other in the face and cried, his sobs pushing out more stomach contents at the g-tube site while I pathetically tried to wipe it up, all the time yelling, "Just stop!" and "I don't know what to do!"

The second time the g-tube got the better of me, Travis and I decided that we needed to get rid of it and began working toward that goal. Despite our best efforts, the site kept leaking, his skin was constantly raw, he always smelled a bit like barf, and he was obviously miserable. Adding to his discomfort was the fact that he had a horrible case of cradle cap and eczema, and he was vomiting at least once a day almost every day. We didn't know what was going on, but we knew we needed to improve James's quality of life so he could begin meeting milestones again.

In December, when he was three months old, we stopped using the g-tube altogether. He thinned out after having become a Buddha-baby in the hospital, but he also started taking a bottle consistently. In February, his neurologist suggested that James's skin problems might be a reaction to the phenobarbital he had been on since birth because of the seizure. Believing James would probably never have another seizure, the neurologist gave us a five-week schedule to wean him off the sedating medication. In March, at six months of age, James was completely off all his medications and had his g-tube removed because it hadn't been used in three months.

Still, he seemed so miserable at times, and his skin was still covered with eczema. He also still vomited frequently. Later that spring, we learned that James has incredibly severe allergies to dairy, nuts, eggs, dust, and cats. We finally had the last piece of the puzzle, which explained those health issues. We began to work to get his allergies under control.

With all of these needed adjustments, James was a new baby. No more throwing up, no more tummy aches, no more irritated, weeping skin. With these changes and the fact that his body had had enough time to rest and recuperate from his traumatic birth, James finally seemed like a completely normal, healthy baby. We watched him meet his milestones, often shaking our heads in disbelief with tears in our eyes. We celebrated all the things he was never supposed to be able to do, and we praised and thanked God.

It was an incredible position to be in: For so long, we had prayed and hoped against hope for a miracle. It took months for us to finally see it, as we waited for milestones and figured out his special medical needs. Now, before our eyes, it was evident that God had answered our prayers. Already James was able to do so much more than he ever should have been able to. It seemed obvious to us that when God brought James back to life, he had done so in such a way that James's body would not only survive, but also thrive. We poured out praise and thanksgiving to God, of course, but we were also so grateful for all the friends, family, and strangers who had interceded for our son, the first and foremost Fulton Sheen.

CHAPTER 17

What the Doctors Said

As Travis and I adjusted to life at home with three children and did our best to care for James, the medical experts who followed his progress were consistently encouraging.

The first great thrill came when three-month-old James had a follow-up MRI. Because he was so young, he needed anesthesia so he would lie still for the test. As everyone prepared for the procedure, the anesthesiologist asked why James was having the MRI. I began my explanation: He had been a stillborn and had been without a pulse for sixty-one minutes following birth.

She immediately interrupted. "You mean sixty-one seconds. You said sixty-one minutes, but you mean a little over one minute."

"No," I said. "He didn't have a pulse for over an hour." She stared at James with wide eyes and then looked back at me. Enjoying the disbelief on her face, I smiled and nodded. She turned back to James, who was lying on the hospital bed while a nurse attached identification bracelets to his arm and foot. The nurse and the doctor watched him kick and grab and smile, and they looked at each other and then back at me. They didn't say it, but "Whoa!" was written all over their faces.

"I know," I said. "He's a miracle." I paused for a moment as they nodded in agreement, and then I continued with his medical history. "He underwent cooling therapy in the NICU, but an MRI done early on at the hospital showed injury to his brain. This follow-up MRI will let us know the lasting effects of the hour he was dead when his brain didn't get oxygen."

Later that month, just a few days before Christmas, the kids and I were visiting my mom when my cellphone rang. Seeing it was our family doctor's office, I asked Mom to watch the kids, and I went into my old bedroom, which now served as my parents' den. I pulled a piece of paper and a pen out of the desk drawer to write down the MRI's results. A flurry of butterflies swarmed my stomach, and the muscles in my shoulders and upper back tightened. I was bracing myself for the worst while hoping for the best.

On the line was a nurse from our family doctor's office; she had the results from the MRI. There was no inflammation and no extra fluid. The blood flow to all areas of his brain was good; all regions and aspects of his brain appeared healthy and normal for his age. I had her repeat everything, writing down the medical jargon to the best of my spelling abilities and noting in simple English what it really meant. Then I read back to her the list and my notes, checking with her that I hadn't missed anything.

"So," I took a deep breath and then continued. "You're telling me that there's nothing wrong with his brain. Is that what you're telling me?"

I could hear the smile in the nurse's voice as she answered, "That's what the results say: no abnormalities."

"Okay, because the first MRI showed that there had been injury to the brain. But there are no longer signs of injury?"

"Let me check with the doctor to make sure I'm reading it correctly, but yes." I heard her question the doctor, and I heard his muffled answer. She came back to the phone: "James's brain is fine. There are no longer signs of injury."

"Well, can you tell me why that would have happened? How could that change have happened?" I knew what I wanted her to say, but I wanted her to be the one to say it.

"I don't know. The human body can do amazing things, but I'd say a miracle."

She had said it. The first MRI had shown obvious injury, but this one showed a perfectly healthy brain. It was a miracle.

I thanked her and ran out of the room, phone and paper in hand.

"Mom! MOM! It was the doctor's office with the MRI results! No brain damage! He's fine! His brain is fine!" She stepped out of the kitchen and looked at me down the hall. She was smiling a big, open-mouthed grin, and she pumped her fists in the air, then clapped her hands together in front of her chest.

"Oh, Bonnie! It's a miracle! Praise God!"

Standing in her living room, I read the list to her. Then she walked toward me, Lydia and Bennet toddling down the hall behind her. As a group we hugged and cheered and jumped up and down. And then I said, "I gotta call Travis!"

Three months later, we were making the rounds for his six-month checkup. Most of the doctors and therapists had tend-ed to James in the NICU and so had witnessed his full medical history, including the results from the latest MRI. The devel-opmental and physical therapists, his neurologist and the devel-opmental pediatrician, all the nurses who took his weight and measured his head circumference, all of them studied him. They watched him hold his own bottle and interact with his siblings and toys. They asked if he could do certain things, they checked off the list of milestones, and they all said the same thing. Over and over, one after another, they would shake their heads and say in a tone just louder than a whisper, "He shouldn't be like this. It's amazing. He's amazing."

I asked our family practitioner his thoughts about James. "It's not a miracle that James is alive — it's amazing, but it's not a miracle. It is a miracle that he's doing as well as he is. He shouldn't be like this. He shouldn't be normal."

By ten months, James was crawling and getting into mis-chief. At eleven months he was assessed by his physical therapist, who wrote, "James is an eleven-month-old who is currently func-tioning at eleven months for gross motor skills and twelve and a half months for fine motor skills." At his one-year follow-up with his neurologist, the doctor was so impressed with James that he would ask a question, look at my son, do a small examination, and then say, "Unbelievable." He repeated those steps numerous times, speaking under his breath to himself and sometimes aloud to me, "Impressive. Amazing. Remarkable. Unbelievable. Quite impressive."

Shortly after James's first birthday, we saw the developmental pediatrician again. In many ways, it felt like our entire family's fate was in his hands. What he said would influence how every other doctor and therapist viewed James. I worried that he would see something that the rest of us did not and that he would continue to leave cerebral palsy as a possibility for James. Worse yet, I was afraid that he'd tell us we had been blinded by hope and that my son did, in fact, right now, have cerebral palsy. With a strong mix of hope and terror, we watched as he examined James. He asked us some questions, wanting to know about milestones and what James did at home. Then, with a big smile on his face and a slight shake of his head, he said: "It's astounding and really, really wonderful. There is nothing to be concerned about. I see no lasting effects from the trauma of his birth."

When we finished making the rounds for all his one-year checkups, James was fully discharged from the care of most of the professionals who had followed him throughout his life so far. The neurologist, physical therapist, developmental pediatrician, and stomach surgeon all felt they had no reason to see him ever again. We finally had the medical support for what we had suspected for quite a while: God had indeed performed a miracle for our son.

At the end of all the appointments, our little family celebrated the good news with a trip to the local ice cream stand. As we ate our chocolate cones, we rejoiced in the power of prayer, our friendship with Fulton Sheen, and the generosity of God.

CHAPTER 18

To Tribunal, or Not to Tribunal

Half-jokingly, friends would ask Travis and me whether we were saving up for a trip to Rome, implying that James's healing would be the miracle leading to Servant of God Fulton J. Sheen's beatification and canonization. We always said the same thing: "Uh, no."

But those friends became more insistent after the results from the follow-up MRI came back saying there was no brain damage. By the time James was four months old, people began to insist that we call the Archbishop Fulton John Sheen Foundation, the official promoter of Sheen's cause for canonization, and tell them our story.

One afternoon, my mom brought it up with me, wanting to know whether I'd told the Sheen Foundation yet. I hadn't.

"Mom, I just don't think I should call. People keep teasing about it being used for Sheen's beatification or canonization miracle but — I mean — come on! We're not going to Rome."

"Bonnie." There was a firmness in her voice. This was mom mode, and I needed to listen, not argue, and do as I was told. "They will want to know. Even if all they do is write it down in a file, they will want to keep track of the fact that people are asking for his intercession and that miracles are happening because of it."

So in the quiet of the afternoon, while Lydia, Bennet, and James napped, I called the foundation and spoke with Sister Ann, a religious sister with whom I was acquainted. After we exchanged pleasantries and caught up, I told her that I wanted to share a story about a miracle that had taken place through Fulton Sheen's intercession. Now, people contact the Sheen Foundation to share stories of their own little miracles every day, and Sister Ann assumed I'd tell a similar tale, something sweet and wonderful but nothing of biblical proportions.

I felt a bit ridiculous telling her the story. My voice shook as I began. I told her about the healthy pregnancy, the homebirth, the stillbirth, the baptism, the ambulance, the emergency room, the confirmation, the NICU, and the MRIs. Without going into too much detail — I didn't want to bog her down — I covered the important points and ended by confirming that James Fulton was alive and well.

When I had finished, Sister Ann barely paused before she asked, "You said he didn't have a pulse for over an hour?"

"Yes, Sister."

"And now he's okay?"

"Yes, Sister."

"Let me get a pencil."

I smiled and chuckled a bit. Obviously, this was not the type of story she was used to hearing. She asked clarifying questions; I gave her more information; and she took notes so she could accurately share the story with the director of the Sheen Foundation, Monsignor Stanley Deptula.

Around this same time, our friend Jenny shared James's story with her friend and confessor — who happened to be the very same Monsignor Deptula. Monsignor became engrossed and asked if we would email him a summary of the events. As the Sheen Foundation reviewed Sister's notes, Monsignor's email, and Jenny's witness, they decided to forward our story to the Roman postulator, Dr. Andrea Ambrosi, who was guiding Sheen's cause for canonization. His guidance would help the Sheen Foundation decide whether or not to open a tribunal — an official investigation into James's alleged miracle.

During the canonization process, the pope is kind of like the judge; the Congregation for the Causes of Saints is like the jury; and the postulator is like the district attorney, who gathers and presents the evidence needed to move the process forward. Even though Dr. Ambrosi had already prepared cases for two alleged miracles through Sheen's intercession, he was intrigued by this story of a baby born dead who came back to life. Aware that we had abundant medical documentation for James's story, he asked the Sheen Foundation to gather more information.

With the postulator's interest piqued, my task was to speak with James's doctors about what they thought of his birth, prognosis, and subsequent development. We wanted to know whether they thought that James's healing was miraculous, but we wanted them to be the ones to say "miracle" first, because we didn't want to "lead the witness," so to speak. Without using the "m" word, I discussed James's health during a private visit with Dr. Corrales, the neonatologist who had been on call the night James was born and had helped care for him in the NICU.

"People are always asking me to explain what happened to James and how it is that he turned out so well. How would you explain it to people?" I asked her.

She leaned forward in her chair, and with a slightly raised voice she pronounced: "He's a miracle! That's all you need to say!"

On her own, without any hints from me, she used the million-dollar word — the one I wanted to hear. She said it: "He's a miracle."

Being completely familiar with James's medical history and knowing how far he'd come, she could think of no plausible medical explanation for why James was the way he was. "Maybe he had excellent CPR the whole time," she offered, though the look on her face and the tone in her voice showed that she wasn't convinced.

"He's a miracle baby," she concluded.

As we received positive feedback from James's six-month checkups, we reported back to the Sheen Foundation. They passed on the information to Dr. Ambrosi who told them to pursue the alleged miracle because it was a "strong case."

Travis and I were thrilled but also completely caught off guard. When we had originally agreed to contact the Sheen

Foundation, we believed they would take a note, say, "Praise God!" and add James's story to a big book that contained many other alleged miracles. Instead, we suddenly found ourselves in a part of the Catholic world that was unfamiliar to us.

Quickly, we were brought up to speed on what had happened with Fulton Sheen's cause so far. In 2002, while Travis and I were still college students, the Diocese of Peoria, Illinois, opened the cause for Archbishop Fulton J. Sheen's canonization. The Congregation for the Causes of Saints then gave Sheen the title "Servant of God," an important step in the investigation of an individual for possible canonization.

Almost immediately, the Sheen Foundation began collecting documentation to support the claim that Archbishop Sheen had lived a life of heroic virtue. It took six years to collect all the witness testimony. At the same time, historians and theologians reviewed the vast number of books and other writings by Archbishop Sheen to ensure that they were consistent with the teachings of the Catholic Church.

In 2006, two fully investigated alleged miracles were sent to Rome to await verification. The postulator held on to them while the Sheen Foundation continued to gather evidence of Sheen's holiness and virtue. In 2008, thousands of pages of testimony to his personal holiness and copies of Sheen's writings were sent to Rome, and Dr. Ambrosi prepared to present a *positio*, a summation of Sheen's life and works, showing Sheen's heroic virtue. On April 15, 2008, the investigation into his heroic virtue was officially opened in Rome with a ceremony at the offices of the

Vatican Congregation for the Causes of Saints.

Travis and I had been fairly oblivious to many of these events. Now we sat on the edge of our seats, reading with rapt attention about how our bishop, Daniel R. Jenky, officially presented a copy of the *positio* to Pope Benedict XVI on May 25, 2011. At their meeting, Pope Benedict expressed an interest in Sheen's cause and commented to Bishop Jenky that he had known and worked with Archbishop Sheen during Vatican II. We were giddy: Pope Benedict knew our Fulton Sheen!

CHAPTER 19

To Tribunal

Meanwhile, back in Illinois, I was gathering medical records. After months of meetings, phone calls, and emails, we finally received word in late July that there would be an official tribunal to investigate our claim that James had been miraculously healed through the intercession of Fulton J. Sheen. As the date approached, the Sheen Foundation walked us through what a Church tribunal would look like. Roles were assigned by Bishop Jenky: an episcopal delegate to guide the process, a medical expert, a notary, a copyist, Dr. Ambrosi the postulator, and a "promoter of justice." I jokingly asked whether the last one wore a cape and a mask. I was told that he did not, just a Roman collar, and that his job would be to ensure that all procedures were followed correctly. Throughout the investigation, they would gather information to prove or disprove that a miracle had, in fact, occurred.

On September 7, 2011, just nine days before James's first

birthday, the tribunal was opened in a private gathering held in the chapel at the diocesan office building. Members of the Sheen Foundation board came from all over the country to be part of the event, as did several of Fulton Sheen's cousins and other relatives. The postulator and his American assistant came from Rome and sat next to Monsignor Deptula and Bishop Jenky in the front of the chapel. Travis and I were happy to see Monsignor Jason Gray, who would serve as the episcopal delegate. We didn't know him personally, but everything we knew of Monsignor Gray made us like him: He was smart, funny, orthodox, and his homilies were never too long. We sat to the side, holding James and feeling greatly out of place.

As the ceremony began, Travis leaned over and whispered in my ear: "I feel like this is too important for us to be here. It feels like we should be in some medieval monastery — it's all just so ancient and mysterious."

It was true. We were sitting in on a secret ceremony, one we could not discuss with others. Witness testimony needed to be preserved from the influence of speculation from the press or general public, so nothing could be discussed while the investigation was happening. We watched as members of the tribunal went to the altar one by one and read an oath written on a document, swearing to pursue the truth throughout the investigation. They signed their names and then set their own seal on the document.

The language of the ceremony was beautiful, and it captured our imaginations. Each participant read out an oath like this one, taken by Bishop Jenky:

> In the name of the Lord, I, Monsignor Daniel R. Jenky,
> Bishop of Peoria, in the Diocesan Inquiry on the alleged
> miracle attributed to the intercession of the Servant of
> God Archbishop Fulton Sheen, do solemnly swear that I
> will faithfully and carefully execute the duty committed
> to me, and I will keep secret all that I may learn during
> said Inquiry. In fulfilling my duty, I will keep before my
> eyes only God and the good of the Church. So help me
> God.

We felt privileged to witness something so rare and so magnificent, and we felt grateful to belong to a Church that is "ever ancient, ever new."

In the following weeks, the tribunal called in sixteen witnesses to give their personal testimonies. Some were friends who could attest to our fondness for Fulton Sheen. They testified that we had called on Sheen to pray for James. Some of the witnesses were the medical professionals who had attended the homebirth and could confirm that James had been a stillborn. Others were nurses and doctors who had cared for James in the hospital and who testified about the seriousness of his condition and what could be expected for his life. Other doctors who had examined James after his discharge discussed how well he was doing.

Travis and I each told our story, separately from one another. I was the first to be interviewed.

I sat at a small conference table. Monsignor Gray sat at the head of the table, wearing his black clerics and white Roman collar. His briefcase leaned against his chair, and a voice recorder sat on the table in front of him, along with a packet containing close to forty questions.

Dr. Louis Varela, a Texas doctor, sat across the table from me. He was sitting in on the interviews to make sure medical questions were clearly stated and sufficiently answered. His voice was soft, his smile was kind, and his eyes portrayed a real interest in hearing, straight from the horse's mouth as it were, the story he had already read.

Monsignor James Kruse sat at the end of the table, opposite Monsignor Gray. Monsignor Kruse is a local priest, and I barely knew him, but I could tell that he was full of energy and joy. He was the promoter of justice and was present to ensure that the Church's Code of Canon Law — the laws and regulations that guide the governance of the Catholic Church — were followed throughout the investigation.

We exchanged pleasantries. I warned the men that I might cry. Then Monsignor Gray hit the record button and began. The first questions were delightfully easy: What's your name? Where do you live? Who are your children? When did you begin asking Fulton Sheen to pray for your baby?

But the longer we spoke, the more difficult the questions became to answer. First they needed to establish evidence for the love and respect my husband and I felt for Fulton Sheen. What had made us turn to him for prayers when it became clear that we needed a miracle to save our baby? Monsignor Gray began to ask about my labor, James's delivery, and everything that happened after. As I answered these questions, Monsignor Gray, Dr. Varela, and Monsignor Kruse would ask clarifying questions in order to ensure that every detail was covered in the quest for the fullness of truth.

I tried to speak with confidence, but I had to fight the lump in my throat and the tears in my eyes. For some reason, I felt like I needed to be brave and tough and keep a stiff upper lip. It's hard to talk about the death and suffering of your child, even after his miraculous recovery.

Toward the end of the interview, Monsignor Gray asked why I thought James came back to life and was now so healthy. I responded that I believed it was a miracle, performed by God, and that Fulton Sheen's prayers had been an important part of it. Monsignor asked if others believed the same thing, and I told him that many of our friends and family and even people who followed us online believed it was a miracle through the intercession of Fulton Sheen. Then he asked if there were any people who believed it wasn't because of Fulton Sheen.

"Yes," I said.

The three men looked a bit alarmed — I don't think they were expecting such a firm answer. Monsignor Gray asked who did not believe it.

Thinking of James's favorite NICU night nurse, speech therapist, and various relatives, I answered, "Protestants. But they still think it's a miracle."

At the end of the two-hour interview, Monsignor Gray thanked me for my time and explained that every witness would be asked the same set of questions to ensure continuity, but I was not to discuss any of the questions with anyone except for the witnesses who had also completed their testimony. We each had our own area of expertise in regard to James's story, and all of us vowed that we were telling the absolute truth.

Once the interviews were typed, each witness — the doctors and nurses, our friends, Travis and I — received a packet with our transcripts. We read through the many pages, made any necessary clarifications or corrections to our testimonies, and then signed the document, stating that it was the truth. If the transcript had to be updated and corrected, the new copy was mailed out for a final review, which we then signed and returned to the tribunal. Every single page of each transcript was stamped and signed by a notary. All of us who testified were vowing to God, the pope, and all the world that we were telling the truth, the whole truth, and nothing but the truth. I've signed many official documents in my life, but nothing seemed as serious as when I signed my name on the final page of that transcript.

The tribunal officially came to a close on the Third Sunday of Advent in 2011, just three short months after it had been opened. While the whole Church rejoices on Gaudete Sunday, we at the Cathedral of Saint Mary of the Immaculate Conception had extra reasons to celebrate. We celebrated the gift of faith, the gift of Fulton Sheen, and the gift of a possible miracle right in our midst.

Standing at the altar, Bishop Jenky took the bundles of medical records and witness testimony that were wrapped in brown paper. He tied them with red ribbon and fastened the ribbon with sealing wax and an official seal. Wrapped around each package was a piece of diocesan stationary that read:

> Enclosed is the true and authentic Transcript and Public Copy in the case of the alleged miraculous healing of James Fulton Engstrom through the intercession of the Servant of God, Archbishop Fulton Sheen.

The document was signed by Monsignor Gray and a notary, who each also stamped the paper with their official seal.

As I took it all in, I was struck by the way in which every step of the process had been dedicated to the truth. In the public eye, the Catholic Church is often considered untrustworthy: full of liars, pedophile priests, and fools who manipulate truth to control the ignorant. That's not what Travis and I experienced. We saw men and women driven by their love of God, their desire to see him glorified, and their commitment to help others to love him, too. We saw good, honest, hardworking priests do everything they could to uncover and understand the truth in every detail of James's story. We worked with diocesan priests and employees who were willing to see all their hard work come to nothing if the medical case for a miracle proved weak, because they knew that anything less than the truth would not honor God.

This sincere dedication to the truth no matter the cost was something we had taken for granted, or perhaps had just never before experienced on such a personal level. To witness it first-hand was a blessing and an affirmation of how dedicatedly good our Church is.

CHAPTER 20

Venerable Fulton J. Sheen

A fter the tribunal's closing Mass, we waited.

In Rome, Dr. Ambrosi and his staff were busy having James's evidence translated into Italian and making other preparations so a medical *positio* on James could be written. Even when the medical *positio* was finished, though, nothing could be done with it until the first *positio* proved Archbishop Fulton Sheen's heroic virtue, allowing his cause to progress to the next step.

So, really, we were waiting on God's timing just as much as we were waiting on translators and copyists. Every once in a while, I would cry out in my prayers, "You're killin' me, Smalls!" (knowing that God would pick up on my reference to the baseball movie *The Sandlot*). We were warned that the Church takes her time, but we were also encouraged — and perhaps naively so — by how quickly things seemed to be happening. Travis and I were excited for things to proceed because, well, it was so exciting! But we were also hoping everything would happen while James was still young.

We have always been convinced that sharing James's story glorifies God, and we've been happy to do so. But we also want to protect our child. We hoped that, for James's sake, the miracle would be approved and Venerable Sheen beatified while James was still a small boy, allowing him to grow up with all of it in his past. We wondered how we would protect him from cameras, well-intentioned strangers, and mean people on the internet when he was old enough to search his name on Google. As long as he was a baby, Travis and I could put ourselves out there in his place, with little being expected from him because of his age. But what if he were in the middle of puberty or his boisterous early twenties when the miracle was approved, and the spotlight turned back on him? To us it felt easier to balance protecting our child and serving the Lord while James was young, so once again we called on Fulton Sheen to help us, to intercede on our behalf so that the timing would all be perfect. Then we willed ourselves to believe that all was working for the good as we waited.

We celebrated Christmas and our fifth wedding anniversary. The kids made valentines and learned about Saint Patrick. We fasted through Lent, feasted through Easter, and in May I gave birth to baby Teresa. Still, we heard nothing about the progress of Sheen's cause for canonization.

But on June 28, 2012, more than a year after Pope Benedict had met Bishop Jenky and expressed his interest in Sheen's cause, the announcement came: Archbishop Fulton J. Sheen had been named "Venerable" by the Holy Father.

That night we celebrated with pizza and ice cream. Now

that the Vatican had officially recognized Sheen's holiness, it was finally time for the postulator to submit one of the three documented, alleged miracles to the office of the Congregation for the Causes of Saints for review. If the congregation and the Holy Father found the submitted alleged miracle to be a true miracle, then Sheen would be beatified, the last step before canonization.

Of course, we hoped that James's story would be the one submitted and approved. Knowing what could lie ahead, we wondered whether God would use our son's miracle to beatify Fulton Sheen. We had started James's life trusting in God's goodness and plan. We had shared James's story with the Sheen Foundation only as a way to honor God's faithfulness and love. We didn't know what God would do next, but we believed that whatever happened would be for his greater glory.

"But it would be so cool if it was James," we both agreed, grinning goofily. "It would be awesome."

On June 29, the Sheen Foundation told us that James's medical *positio* would be officially submitted to the Congregation for the Causes of Saints. The two other alleged miracles would be held by Dr. Ambrosi as backups. We continued our celebration while trying to remain cautious. There was always a chance that a doctor, theologian, cardinal, or even the pope himself would not agree that James's recovery was a true miracle. Instead of focusing on the "what if's" we continued to pray for Venerable Sheen's canonization as the waiting game started all over again.

CHAPTER 21

Unanimous Approval

We waited almost two years. James turned two. He became a big brother again when Joseph was born. We celebrated his third birthday with a Mickey Mouse cake. He started preschool. Life kept chugging along, and all the while we prayed for Fulton Sheen's cause, never really knowing what was happening with it over in Rome.

Finally, in the winter of 2014, we heard rumblings. The seven medical experts who advise the Congregation for the Causes of Saints were reviewing James's *positio* and were so intrigued that they asked for an update on James's health. He was now four years old. We took him to the doctor for a full physical, and our physician then provided a letter testifying to James's health and declaring that he saw no lasting effects from the trauma at James's birth.

More time passed. Then, early in the morning of March 6, 2014, I received a phone call from Monsignor Deptula: Later that morning the press would be notified that the seven medical experts had unanimously approved the alleged miracle, affirming that no natural cause could be found for James's recovery. I did a little happy dance in the living room, giddily called Travis to share the news with him, and then bundled up my kids and loaded them into the van to take Lydia and James to school.

After dropping off the two, I headed to the store to do some shopping. In an aisle filled with clocks and picture frames, I got a follow-up call. The press release had gone out, and I could now tell anyone I wanted. Fist-pumping in the air, I called my mom. On the way home, I passed our parish and my daughter's school. I was bursting to share the good news with people, so I stopped at the parish office and asked after the priests. They were both hearing confessions for the school kids, so I went to the church, told the teachers what was happening, and cut in front of a third grader.

Slipping into the confessional, I said to our associate pastor, "Father. This is Bonnie Engstrom." Without pausing for his response, I quickly continued: "I'm not here to confess; I just wanted to let you know as soon as possible that the medical experts have approved James's miracle! It's going to advance! We're one step closer!"

Through the grille, I could see his smile. "That's great! Wow!"

We chatted in the standard hushed tones of the confessional, said our goodbyes, and I stepped out to see our main pastor enter the church. I approached him before he slipped into his confessional and shared the good news with him, too. He was thrilled. While the alleged miracle was not officially approved by the Church, this was such an important step toward that final goal.

The second step came just three months later, on June 17, 2014. That morning I once again received an early morning phone call from Monsignor Deptula. Later that day, a new press release would go out: The team of theological advisers to the Congregation of the Causes of Saints had also unanimously approved

the miracle. After studying the *positio*, they had concluded that the miracle had happened because of faith in Jesus Christ and the prayers of Fulton Sheen.

Travis and I were thrilled. It was all so exciting, because we knew how important it was. This approval brought Archbishop Sheen's cause one step closer to beatification, and we knew how much the Church would benefit from Sheen's sainthood. Every time we shared James's story and spoke of Fulton Sheen, we saw how people were moved. Hearts opened, faith grew, praise poured out. We couldn't help but cheer and celebrate this advancement. With Travis looking on and laughing, I clapped my hands, pumped my fists, raised my hands to God, and called out, "BOOM SHAKALAKA!"

That night we dined on Chinese takeout and ice cream sundaes.

***

One month later, in July 2014, I was preparing to travel out of state when I received one more phone call. The cause had been closed. It was not public knowledge, as the Diocese of Peoria and the Sheen Foundation were trying to solve the issue and reopen the cause out of the public eye, but it was closed. I kept the secret for the rest of the summer, until September came and I no longer had to do so.

In September 2014, the Sheen Foundation and the Diocese of Peoria publicly announced that the cause was closed and would remain so until further notice. Our family and friends hoped and prayed that everything would be resolved quickly and without scandal, but after more than four years of waiting, we came to understand that our schedule was not the same as God's perfect timing.

Finally, in late June 2019, the cause reopened. Archbishop Sheen's mortal remains were brought back to St. Mary's Cathedral in Peoria, Illinois, where he served Mass as a boy and was ordained as a young man. Countless pilgrims streamed through the large, heavy doors of the cathedral to welcome him home and pray before his tomb. I was one of them. As I knelt in prayer, I let out one deep sigh after another. With each exhale I felt a weight lift off my chest and gratitude settle deeper in my heart. For the good of the Church and the glory of God, the Sheen Foundation could once again progress with Venerable Fulton J. Sheen's cause for canonization.

With the cause officially out of the archives, the *positio* on James's miracle was almost immediately approved by the cardinals who sit on the Congregation for the Causes of Saints. With their approval it was then submitted to the Holy Father, Pope

Francis, for his review. On July 6, 2019, I was awakened by the sound of my phone vibrating from a notification. I had been tagged in a post by a friend whose joy could not be contained, even at 6:20 in the morning. The previous day, Pope Francis had approved the miracle for Archbishop Sheen's beatification.

With that news I threw on some clothes and headed to morning Mass, offering it up in thanksgiving. On the way home, I picked up donuts, chocolate milk, and mochas. That breakfast was only the beginning; we celebrated for days.

Chapter 22

A Normal Boy

If you saw my kids and me at the park today, you would never be able to guess which one should, by all accounts, be severely disabled. If you stood behind us in the checkout line, you would never know that one of them had been dead for more than an hour. Unless you knew us and our story, you'd never suspect that my blue-eyed boy was another Lazarus. In fact, unless you saw the two scars on his should-have-been-amputated leg, or the g-tube scar on his belly, you would never assume he had any kind of medical history at all.

Of course, a miracle doesn't mean there can't be other problems. One can be healed of cancer and still have a stutter or heart disease, and this is true for James. He still struggles with severe allergies, and he has other challenges, too. But none of those difficulties lessen what God has done. It is remarkable that he is alive. That James went through so much as an infant and has no significant issues: inconceivable! And trust me, there are people who do not believe. But we believe that God restored him to life and did so fully. We believe that James just might be exactly who God intended him to be before the trauma of his birth. We also wonder, though, whether any of his struggles are a result of everything he went through at birth, in the NICU, and in follow-up procedures, and if they remain for a greater reason. Saint Augustine once wondered if in heaven "we shall see on the bodies of the Martyrs the traces of the wounds which they bore for Christ's name: because it will not be a deformity, but a dignity in them."* We don't know, but we wonder whether it is the same for James. James was dead for sixty-one minutes after he was born. Yet today he chows down on a hamburger, asks to watch *Star Wars*, and rides a two-wheeled bicycle. None of this should have been possible, given the circumstances of his birth; yet, I see the reality of it every single day. I know he is a miracle.

---

* Saint Augustine quoted in Thomas Aquinas *Summa Theologiae*, III, 54, 4.

God Set the Table

At times I still ask myself, "Why did all this happen, and why did it happen to us?" The simple answer is, I don't know — but to the best of my understanding, everything has been as God wanted it to be. As I once explained it to a friend, "God set the table." God put down the linens, laid out the dishes, arranged the flatware, and set out the food. He invited me and my family to join him. All we did was show up and sit down in the chairs he pulled out for us.

People have often commented about how strong we were throughout everything, and I know from the outside it looked like Travis and I were carrying crosses of herculean proportions. But by the grace of God, the yoke was easy and the burden was light. Our greatest pain was in watching our small son suffer; the countless heel pricks, tests, surgeries, procedures … it broke our hearts over and over again. But we trust that James's suffering was redemptive — hopefully ours was, too — and that great good will come about because of it.

Fulton Sheen once said: "Miracles are no cure for unbelief. Some would not believe even though one were to rise daily from the dead. ... No sign could be wrought which would bring complete conviction, for the will can refuse assent to what the intellect knows to be true."* That is true, but I know that James's story has touched people, sometimes in profound ways. It has led people to pick up books and listen to preaching by Fulton Sheen. It has brought people back to prayer and given hope to the hopeless. James's story has inspired people to seek out Jesus Christ.

We have always likened James's story to the story of Lazarus, for there is much we identify with as we read it. That Christ would allow both his friend and my son to lie dead while he waited for the perfect timing. The way that Martha, Travis, and I all believed that Jesus is "the Christ, the Son of God" (Jn 11:27), but didn't know what he would do in our time of crisis. The way that we all worried about the damage and decay that had been done to our loved ones' bodies. Above all else, though, for me, the deepest connection is that for James and Lazarus, it was Christ's victory over death that won life for them.

Bishop Sheen once preached: "Our Lord went to the tomb of Lazarus ... and our Lord rose Lazarus from the dead. Our Lord wept when he rose Lazarus from the dead; he wept because he was indignant of death. Where does death come from? It comes

---

* Fulton J. Sheen, *Life of Christ*, reprint (San Francisco: Ignatius Press, 2018), 364.

from sin! It comes from the devil! His resurrection will be the eventual cure of all death, and he wept because he was angry at what evil had brought into the world.'"

It was Jesus Christ who brought James Fulton back to life. It was Christ's death and resurrection that conquered death once and for all (cf. Rom 6:10). I do not know why it happened this way. The only answer I can give is probably the only answer I should be concerned with: the glory of God.

---

* Fulton J. Sheen, "The Death of Lazarus," *Sign of Contradiction: Good Friday and Beyond*, produced by Casscom Media, January 16, 2013.

Appendix 1

Timeline of Fulton J. Sheen's Life
and Canonization Process

1895
May 8, born in El Paso, Illinois, to Newton and Delia (Fulton) Sheen. Baptized Peter John.

1900
Moved with his family to Peoria, Illinois, so he and his three brothers could attend St. Mary's Cathedral School.

1909
Began high school at the Spalding Institute in Peoria, Illinois.

1913
Enrolled in seminary.

1919
September 20, ordained a priest for the Diocese of Peoria. At

his ordination, he consecrated himself to Mary and promised God to make a daily Eucharistic holy hour, which he did faithfully for the rest of his life.

1920

Spent the next four years furthering his education at the Catholic University of America in Washington, D.C., the Sorbonne University in Paris, the Pontifical University of Saint Thomas Aquinas (Angelicum) in Rome, and the University of Louvain in Belgium. At Louvain, Sheen became the first American to receive the Cardinal Mercier Prize for International Philosophy. He also attained the Aggrege degree with outstanding distinction.

1925

Served at St. Patrick's in inner-city Peoria for nine months, during which he revitalized the parish.

1926

Began teaching theology, philosophy, and religion at the Catholic University of America in Washington, D.C., where he would remain until 1950.

1930

"The Catholic Hour," Sheen's national radio broadcast, began. The radio show continued for the next twenty-two years and reached an estimated four million listeners.

1934
Became Very Reverend Monsignor.

1935
Became Right Reverend Monsignor.

1950
Named the national director of the Society for the Propagation of the Faith, a position he held until 1966.

1951
Consecrated a bishop in Rome on June 11.

1952
Began his famous television series "Life Is Worth Living" for which he won an Emmy Award for Most Outstanding Television Personality. The program reached an estimated twenty million viewers each week and ran successfully until 1957.

1962
Attended all of Vatican II sessions in Rome, ending in 1965.

1966
Named bishop of the Diocese of Rochester, New York, on October 26.

1969

Resigned as bishop of Rochester after three difficult years. Was named archbishop of the Titular See of Newport (Wales) by Pope Paul VI. Began an active retirement of writing and preaching.

1979

Met Pope Saint John Paul II on October 3. The pope embraced Sheen and told him, "You have written and spoken well of the Lord Jesus. You are a loyal son of the Church!"

Fulton Sheen died in his New York City apartment on December 9 at the age of eighty-four.

2002

Sheen's cause for canonization officially opened by the Congregation for the Causes of Saints on September 14. Sheen was given the title Servant of God. The cause was promoted by the Catholic Diocese of Peoria, Illinois.

2006

Two tribunals were held to investigate alleged miracles through the intercession of Fulton Sheen. Their findings were sent to Rome.

2008

A closing Mass was held at St. Mary's Cathedral in Peoria, Illinois, on February 3 to mark the ending of the inquiry into the life and works of Fulton Sheen. Dr. Andrea Ambrosi, postulator for the cause, was commissioned by Bishop Daniel Jenky to carry the boxes containing copies of Sheen's writings and thousands of pages of testimony to the Congregation for the Causes of Saints in Rome.

On April 15, the investigation into Sheen's heroic virtue was officially opened in Rome with a ceremony at the office of the Congregation for the Causes of Saints.

2010

James Fulton Engstrom was delivered at home on September 16. He had no pulse for sixty-one minutes and was considered a stillborn. As doctors prepared to call time of death, his heart began to beat again, though he was given a very grim prognosis. During the sixty-one minutes he was nonresponsive; and, throughout his hospital stay, friends and family asked for a miraculous healing through the intercession of Archbishop Fulton Sheen.

2011

The *positio* on the life and works of Archbishop Sheen was presented to the Holy Father, Pope Benedict XVI, by Bishop Jenky on May 25 during a visit to Rome.

On September 7, a tribunal was opened to investigate the alleged miraculous healing of James Fulton Engstrom through the intercession of Fulton J. Sheen.

On September 16, a healthy James Fulton Engstrom turned one year old.

On December 11, after three months of interviewing witnesses and gathering information, the tribunal into the alleged healing of James Fulton was closed at a Mass at the Cathedral of Saint Mary of the Immaculate Conception in Peoria, Illinois.

2012
On June 28, Pope Benedict XVI declared Fulton Sheen "Venerable," bringing Sheen one step closer to canonization. The Sheen Foundation submitted the medical *positio* into James Fulton's alleged miracle to the office of the Congregation for the Causes of Saints.

2014
The medical experts who advise the Congregation for the Causes of Saints unanimously approved James Fulton's alleged miracle on March 6, affirming that no natural cause could be found for his recovery.

On June 17, the theological advisers to the Congregation of the Causes of Saints unanimously approved the alleged miracle, affirming that it had happened because of faith in Jesus Christ and the prayers of Fulton Sheen.

2019

On June 27, Archbishop Fulton J. Sheen's remains were moved from New York to the Cathedral of St. Mary in Peoria, Illinois.

On July 6, Pope Francis approved the miracle, opening the way for Fulton Sheen's beatification.

Appendix 2

The Canonization Process:
An Overview

From my first contact with the Archbishop Fulton John Sheen Foundation and all the way through the writing of this book, I've learned an awful lot about the canonization process, including how much most of us — Catholics and non-Catholics alike — misunderstand or simply don't know. Here, I offer a simple overview to help illustrate and clarify the steps of the process.

Let's use a holy guy named Pete as an example.

SERVANT OF GOD

+ At least five years after Pete's death, a group of people who believe that Pete was a model Christian and is now in heaven gather and approach a diocese that has a connection to Pete to take up his cause.

+ If the diocese agrees, then under the direction of the bishop, it begins to gather preliminary evidence to show that Pete was a holy, orthodox man.

+ This evidence is presented to the Congregation for the Causes of Saints in Rome; if recommended by the congregation, Pete is declared a "Servant of God." Then, a postulator is assigned to gather more evidence and guide the cause.

VENERABLE

+ If an organization has not yet been founded to promote Pete's canonization, that usually happens at this point. Then, the diocese, the organization, and the postulator work together to collect any and all of Pete's writings, such as journals, letters, books, published articles, etc. They also interview witnesses under oath, gathering testimony from people who personally knew Pete and can attest to the ways in which he grew in holiness, loved God, was faithful to the teachings of the Catholic Church, and displayed heroic virtue.

+ This information is gathered by the postulator and written into a *positio*, or position paper, that aims to prove Pete's heroic virtue.

+ The *positio* is presented to the Congregation for the Causes of Saints and is reviewed by three groups of people: theologians; the bishops and cardinals who sit on the Congregation for the Causes of Saints; and then the pope. The *positio* must be given a positive recommendation in order to reach the pope for his approval.

+ If the pope sees proof of heroic virtue, then Pete will be named "Venerable."

BLESSED

+ Once Pete is named Venerable, an alleged miracle can be presented to the Congregation for the Causes of Saints. Let's say someone has allegedly been healed of cancer because of Pete's prayers.

+ The alleged miracle will be thoroughly investigated by a team of experts during an official tribunal. All official records surrounding the event, such as medical records, are attained and processed, and witness testimony is gathered under oath.

+ Tribunal findings are given to the postulator, who prepares the medical *positio* to prove that a true miracle did occur and that it happened because of the intercession of Pete.

+ The medical *positio* is presented to the Congregation for the Causes of Saints, and it again goes through three groups.

Doctors and theologians will evaluate all the medical evidence to confirm that the patient really was dying of cancer with no potential cure when Pete's intercession was sought. It must also be determined that the patient was then cured; there is no medical explanation for it; and the healing was spontaneous, instantaneous, complete, and lasting. The bishops and cardinals of the congregation and, finally, the pope assess the *positio*, looking for the same things.

+ The pope declares the healing truly miraculous. Pete is beatified and now goes by the name Blessed Pete.

+ A feast day is now assigned for Pete, but it is not on the Church's calendar for the whole world; it appears only in areas that would have a connection and devotion to Pete, such as the diocese that is promoting his cause.

SAINT

+ A second alleged miracle, preferably from after the beatification, is now needed. It goes through all the same steps as the alleged miracle for the beatification.

+ If at any time up through this point information is found to prove that Pete was not a godly man, or it was not his prayers that brought about the first miracle, then all titles will be taken away and the cause is stopped. If that is not the case with Pete, then …

+ Upon review, the pope declares this second alleged miracle a true miracle, and Pete is canonized, becoming Saint Pete.

+ Saint Pete's feast day may now be added to the calendar for the universal Church. Churches and other Catholic institutions may now bear Saint Pete's name, and the faithful can now honor and celebrate Saint Pete freely.

ACKNOWLEDGMENTS

There are so many people who have played an important role in our family's story of James's miracle and in the writing of this book.

To begin, we should all be grateful to Cindy Cavnar and Mary Beth Baker whose work editing the book improved every single page and surely freed many poor souls from purgatory.

I'm also grateful to Dr. Shana Freehill, Kelli Dohman-Schmidler, and Joel Geisz who all read through the book at various stages and made sure my medical explanations and jargon usage were correct.

A huge thank you to Teri Ehrenhardt, Jen Rokey, Grete Veliz, Lucy Twait, Sylvie Twait, Lisa Hines, Mary Beth Knott, and all the women and children of Saint Luke's moms' group. I never would have gotten here without their friendship, prayers, and free babysitting.

Jenna Guizar, Beth Davis, and Nell O'Leary have my unending appreciation for helping me to thrive as the folksy daughter of God that I am and for nurturing me as a writer.

I am blessed to be part of a fun, supportive online

community, and many of those women have become dear friends. That seems weird to so many, but, frankly, it is the best. I am grateful to every person who has read my blog, followed me on Instagram, and come to my talks. In a special way, though, I want to say thank you to Haley Stewart, Christy Isinger, Kathryn Whitaker, Kendra Tierney, Mandi Richards, Sarah Ortiz, Abbey Davis Dupuy, Kelly Mantoan, and Ashley Strukel.

I praise God for the circle of friends who have enriched our lives in unfathomable ways and walked with us for many years. Among them are Sister Mariam Caritas, SV, Katie Bogner, Matt and Liz Vander Vennet, and Nick and Mia Handell. Additionally, it is a joy and a gift to live out my vocation alongside friends like the Stevenarts, Codys, Geiszes, Gorsages, Berberichs, Hattons, Rademachers, and Hornings.

Special thanks to Christine Spanhook, Bill and Ginny Hexamer, Charlie and Jamie Blanchard, Kristina Russell, Megan Stevenart, Patti Geisz, and Ruth Cody for all your support.

I am so grateful to all the medical personnel who have cared for James: the first responders and paramedics from Goodfield, Congerville, and Eureka, the staff of the OSF Saint Francis Emergency Department, the staff of the OSF Children's Hospital, and Early Intervention specialists and therapists. I am also indebted to the priests who cared for James and our entire family, including Monsignor Michael Bliss, Father Joseph Donton, Father Nathan Cromly, Father Eugene Radosevich, Father Gary Caster, Father Stephen Willard, and Father Johnathan Steffen.

To my Mom, thank you for insisting that I call the Sheen

Foundation and tell them about James's miracle. I would have let the story sit in the archives of my blog were it not for you. To you and Dad, Grandma and Grandpa Wernsman, Grandma and Grandpa Fandel, Deb and Jeff, Doug and Karl, Bart and Meg: Thank you for your love, support, and encouragement.

To my kids, Peter, Lydia, Bennet, James, Teresa, Joseph, Thomas, Miriam, and Stephen, you make me so happy. I love being your mom. I love you.

Travis, thank you for your faith, your love, your leadership, your sacrifices. I love you, and I am so glad you are my husband. There's no way I could have gone through all of this without you. You are the best.

O my Jesus, I thank You, I love You, I adore You. This is for You.

About the Author

Bonnie L. Engstrom is a popular Catholic blogger and speaker. She loves to bake, putz about her yard, and tell her kids to tidy up the house. She is a regular contributor to Blessed Is She, writes at her website (www.bonnieengstrom.net), and spends too much time on Instagram. She lives in central Illinois with her husband and eight children, and enjoys peace and quiet.

Prayer to Obtain a Favor through the Intercession of
ARCHBISHOP FULTON J. SHEEN

Eternal Father,
You alone grant us every blessing in heaven and on earth, through the redemptive mission of your Divine Son, Jesus Christ, and by the working of the Holy Spirit. If it be according to your will, glorify your servant, Archbishop Fulton J. Sheen, by granting the favor I now request through his prayerful intercession, (state your intention). I make this prayer confidently through Jesus Christ, our Lord.
Amen.